Just Si

*A scientific a_
of Genesis 1 to 11*

Paul Taylor

J6D Publications

i

Published by:
J6D Publications
PO Box 166
Bridgend CF31 9AB
Wales

ISBN: 0-9549500-1-1

Contents

Dedicated to my father, Frank Taylor, 1927 – 2001. Everything I have ever achieved, has been by the grace of God, but in large measure through the sacrifices that Dad made.

Foreword

By Pastor T. Owen Dando

Christian truth has been attacked and misinterpreted ever since the commencement of the Christian era. The persecution of Christians by pagan Rome from 100AD to 313AD issued in the martyrdom of many who maintained their allegiance to Christ.

The hierarchical and liturgical developments of the Roman Catholic church resulted in the pure doctrine of the New Testament becoming contaminated with heresy, the simple but sacred ordinances of Baptism and the Lord's Supper replaced by sacerdotalism, and the purity of spiritual living lost in moral corruption.

Into this quagmire of apostasy came the dawn of the Reformation, revolting against the supremacy of Papacy and reviving and re-establishing the doctrines of the Christian faith as revealed in the scriptures.

But darker days were to follow the daylight of the Reformation. The foes of Christianity, in the forms of Higher-Criticism, Materialism, Darwinism and Marxism were to cause havoc to the Christian faith during the 19th Century and into the 20th. Perhaps the most subtle of these is Darwinism. Although Higher-Criticism was related more to biblical theology, with Materialism and Marxism relating to the religious, social and political institutions of society, Darwinism and evolutionary thought not only entered into the sphere of theology, but also into the educational system. It has entered from the lower class of educational curricula to the higher sphere of academic thought in universities and colleges and its prevalence in modern thought is beyond all dubiety, undermining the early structure of life belief in a Divine Creator.

However, many scholarly and scientific contenders for Creationism – many who were once ardent believers and expositors of the theory of evolution – are now actively engaged in expounding the doctrine of Creation, as revealed in the early chapters of the Book of Genesis.

It is therefore with great pleasure that I accepted the invitation of the author of this book to review its contents, especially with reference to scriptural application. The book is a careful analysis of the biblical account of the creation of the universe. But coupled to this, it must be noted that the author seeks, not only to bring clarity of thought relative to Creation, but also the simplicity of truth relative to man's redemption.

T. Owen Dando
January 2005

Preface

It could be said that this book is a distillation of my thoughts on creationism over the last thirty-something years, because that is how long I have been involved in the study of creationism, and in particular the wonderful book of Genesis.

I was studying for my A-levels in the mid-to-late Seventies, and was working Saturdays in a Christian bookshop in Ashton-under-Lyne. I had been a Christian about a year. Suddenly, the implications of my new faith on my science A-levels were going to become very real. In one of the quiet moments in the shop – of which there were many – I idly picked up a booklet from a new Christian organisation called the Biblical Creation Society. This was the first issue of their former journal, Biblical Creation. I was astounded to read that there were actually people in the world, who did not believe in Darwin's Theory of Evolution. To place the event in its context, there was a major TV series showing at the time, called "Life on Earth", made by TV evangelist for evolutionism, David Attenborough. I took the booklet to the shop manager to express my surprise. He informed me that he didn't believe in evolution, either. The substance of his argument was staggering. He gave me a number of detailed scientific reasons why evolution could not have happened. I immediately understood the import of what he was saying. If I was to accept his arguments, I was to be on a collision course for the rest of my scientific career, on which I was only just about to embark.

The shop manager recommended a book for me to read. It was called "Evolution or Creation" by Professor H. Enoch. As I read through this book, I was impressed by the scientific integrity of the arguments. Not only that, but the book showed that there were profound theological problems with believing in evolution.

I was quickly convinced of the arguments. I showed the book to my father. He read it, and was also quickly convinced.

Thirty years on, and I am more convinced than ever that the world and the universe came about exactly as God said so. I am utterly convinced of the correctness of Genesis. In that shop in Ashton, I realised that if Genesis was true, then the rest of the Bible was true too. It was finding out the truth about Genesis that turned me into a thoroughly Bible-believing evangelical.

Another book that I read in my early Christian life was "The Genesis Record" by Henry Morris. Morris described his book as "a scientific and devotional commentary on Genesis." There was nothing else like that book. Here was a man, who had meditated on the spiritual significance of Genesis, and had written down his thoughts, systematically, including all the relevant contemporary science.

Science has moved on. Creation scientists have done much new research that casts a different light on the scientific consequences of Genesis. The spiritual significance of Genesis remains the same, however. It is as true now as it was then. Though I cannot claim to be in Dr. Morris's class, and indeed I have tackled only eleven chapters, where Morris tackled the whole book, I have thought for the last five years that a new devotional yet scientific work is needed. I have attempted to provide such a work, drawing on a great deal of contemporary creation science, but giving my own opinions on the merits of each piece of research.

There are many people that I need to thank, who have helped this book to emerge. I am particularly grateful to my children, Gemma, Adam and Jack, always ready with an eager, critical eye, to check up on Dad's opinions. I am especially grateful to Pastor Owen Dando, retired pastor and Bible college teacher, who has painstakingly checked both theology and spelling! His enthusiastic support for this project has moved me greatly, and I am honoured that he has agreed to contribute the foreword to this book. My late father was interested in the project, and it is to him that the work is dedicated.

Despite so much assistance, there may still be errors or omissions. If there are, then they are the fault of this author alone.

Paul F. Taylor, B.Sc., M.Ed.
Bridgend, December 2004

1. In the beginning, God

Read Genesis 1:1

Genesis is a Greek word. It means *beginnings*. Although the Old Testament was written in Hebrew, there was a Greek translation of the Old Testament called the Septuagint, translated about 280 to 200 BC. In this work, the first book is called Genesis.

As a Greek word, elements of Genesis appear in English words, especially technical words. Thus, *genetics* is a study of species' origins. We see the word also in such English words as *generation,* and *genealogy*.

Many people will start to read the Bible from Genesis, because it is the first book. If we made no consideration of any studies outside the Bible, we would expect Genesis to lay down the foundations for beliefs, history and doctrine in the rest of the Bible. It is my contention that it is impossible to understand the rest of the Bible, while ignoring this foundational book.

Yet there are many scholars today, who attempt to explain away the book of Genesis. It is described by many as a myth, as legend, as moral teaching, as allegory or as literature or poetry. Indeed, it is probably not an exaggeration to say that most evangelical scholars have given up on a literal, six twenty-four-hour period creation of the world less than ten thousand years ago, in favour of theories, which attempt to harmonise millions of years into the Genesis account. It will be one of the purposes of this study to challenge such aberrations of Biblical interpretation. I sometimes spend time in Christian bookshops, thumbing through the initial few pages of books, to see what position on the creation account is taken by authors. So that there is no confusion, let me set out my belief on this matter right now. This might not be the scholarly way of treating an argument. Some of you want me to examine all sides of the argument first, then tentatively come down off the fence. I believe that the position I take is inherently sound, and have not been afraid to argue the issues elsewhere in this study. But for now, let's make a statement, so that those of you scanning the first couple of pages can find what you want to see.

I believe the entire Bible to be the word of God, authoritative, sufficient, complete and inerrant. In this, I include the book of Genesis. I take the Bible at face value. Since the Bible says that God created the world in just six days, and rested on the seventh, that is what I believe. I accept that these days were literally twenty-four hour periods of time. I believe that there are few, if any gaps in the genealogies – I can accept none in the genealogies of Genesis 5, or 1 Chronicles 1. Thus I believe the world to be *young*, compared to the millions and billions of years usually quoted. I take the Earth to be about six thousand years, though I could possibly stretch to ten thousand at most. I still think six thousand is far more likely. Despite describing this as a *Young Earth* position, I personally think that 6000 years is a very long time, and adequately explains verses in the Bible, which refer to the Earth as ancient. Six thousand years is pretty ancient to me. I do not accept pseudo-creationist theories, therefore, such as Progressive Creationism, Day-Age theory, the Gap Theory, Theistic Evolution, or any other idea, which waters down a belief in the literal, historical truth of Genesis.

There! I've said it all. I hope you will accept that these ideas are not some sort of blind faith. I will return to every one of those statements and justify them, Biblically, Scientifically, or both.

The question in a study such as this is always "where shall we start our study?" I have been speaking and writing on creationism for well over twenty years. I used to start by tackling the science, showing that evolution is wrong. More recently, I have come to the view that the main problem in today's church is a lack of belief in the Bible itself, so I now tend to start from the Bible's account, and build the argument from there.

But how does Genesis itself begin the account. "In the beginning, God…" This powerful set of four words tells us:

- God is central to everything.
- God was before everything.
- Everything had a beginning.
- God was there before that beginning.
- God is the key subject matter of the universe.

We can say nothing about anything in the Bible without reference to God. But this phrase goes further. It declares that we can say nothing about anything, anywhere without reference to God.

6

Thomas Aquinas argued a two-storey model of the universe. This separation can be represented by diagram.

<u>**Grace**</u>

Nature

This diagram can be more fully expressed in the following example, taken from Schaeffer (1976) p55.[1]

Grace, the higher	*God the Creator*; heaven and heavenly things; the unseen and its influence on the earth; *unity*, or universals or absolutes which give existence and morals meaning
Nature, the lower	*the created*; earth and earthly things; the visible and what happens normally in the cause-and-effect universe; what man as man does on the earth; *diversity*, or individual things, the particulars, or the individual acts of man

It is no exaggeration to say that Aquinas's model of the universe has had a profound and overwhelming influence on Western thought, right up to the present day. The result of this is to divorce God from His creation. It relegates all western scientific thought to the lower storey. It is possible that some academics will allow us the study of the spiritual, but these studies are confined to the upper storey, and have no relevance to the world in which we live.

If modern scientific thinking allows for a god at all, it is a lower-storey god. This type of God is described by C.S. Lewis – and you thought he only wrote books about lions, witches and wardrobes! Lewis describes the difference between Nature and Supernature in his book,

---

[1] Schaeffer, F.A. *How Should We Then Live?* The Rise and Decline of Western Thought and Culture, Westchester, (Crossway, 1976), p55

7

Miracles, in which he describes a type of neo-Aquinianism.

> Naturalism, without ceasing to be itself, could admit a certain kind of God. The great interlocking event called Nature might be such as to produce at some stage a great cosmic consciousness, an indwelling 'God' arising from the whole process as human mind arises (according to the Naturalists) from human organisms. A Naturalist would not object to that sort of God. The reason is this. Such a God would not stand outside Nature or the total system, would not be existing 'on his own.'[2]

This type of God would be acceptable to physicists, like Frank Tipler. Tipler developed the so-called *Anthropic Principle*, in which he describes how he believes the universe could only have evolved along a path, which leads to the way it is now. Any other outcome would have been impossible. Although this is not a philosophy that I can embrace, convinced as I am in the truth of God's word, it is interesting that this new cosmology puts Man back at the centre of the universe, from which he was so rudely removed. Tipler argues that there must be a convergence point for all space, time and mass, which he calls the *Omega Point*. This Omega Point, once conceived in this way, then takes on the attributes of God. He says "The logically necessary histories collectively comprising the whole of reality can be regarded as 'emanating' from the Omega Point in his/her transcendence."[3]

The Bible sets itself against the centuries of Aquinianist teaching in these first four powerful words, "In the beginning, God..." The Bible knows nothing of a two storey separation. Such a model is found nowhere in scripture; it is rather the application of Greek thought to theology, which has allowed such thinking to predominate.

There are too many pastors and teachers today, who tell us that we just need to trust in Jesus – it doesn't matter what we believe about Genesis. But the truth of the Bible stands or falls on these first four words. Either we believe God was there in the beginning, or we don't. You see, the early chapters of Genesis touch on real science. There are those today who believe that science has disproved the Bible. It is because of modern theories, which are opposed to what the beginning of

---

[2] Lewis, C.S. *Miracles,* (Collins, 1947), p12
[3] Tipler, F.J. *The Physics of Immortality,* (Macmillan, 1994), p264

the Bible says. But the Bible doesn't start to argue back. It is rightly said that the Bible is not a scientific text book. After all, text books are re-written frequently. The Bible remains the same, because it is God's word to the world. The Bible is not meant to be the book that argues for the existence of God – that's our job. The Bible is rather the book, through which we observe and interpret the world. We are meant to start from the Bible. Once we make this start, we observe that our scientific facts, as we get to learn them, fall into place.

After all, what is the Bible's great statement about the existence, or otherwise, of God.

> The fool has said in his heart, "There is no God." They are corrupt, they have done abominable works. There is none who does good. (Ps. 14:1)

The word translated as fool does not carry quite the same meaning as the English. It refers to someone who is *morally* deficient, as noted by the phrase "They are corrupt". There is, therefore, a *moral* wisdom about believing in God.

That is why the Bible challenges us to believe in God in its first four words. At stake here is our entire belief system. If we don't believe in the truth of the book of Genesis, then there is no basis for our belief in the *morality* taught by the Bible. The Ten Commandments become a waste of time, as does our belief in the Resurrection. And without our belief in the Resurrection, then, in Paul's words, "If in this life only we have hope in Christ, we are of all men the most pitiable." (1 Corinthians 15:19)

These four words demonstrate to us the fact of God's existence, and the futility of believing otherwise. Moreover, they state that God was there "In the beginning", so He was there before the creation of the world. This takes Him outside Nature, and makes Him transcendent, as well as immortal. The four words tell us that everything else, other than God, had a beginning, and that God was the Creator of everything else. There was thus a beginning to time itself. It is difficult to understand a world without Time, but clever physicists, like Stephen Hawking, have tried to get us to do so, so there is no reason for Christians to doubt the beginning of Time. However, our Beginning is not the Beginning of the New Physics, as espoused by Hawking and others. They believe that the universe began in a Big Bang. Thus the universe was once concentrated into one spot, that exploded. Much thought has gone into the mechanism of what matter might be like, in such a Big Bang. Hawking is well known for his "popular" style book, A Brief History of Time, which many have on their bookshelves, but which few understand. This is a shame, because God wants us to understand the Beginning easily. There was no Big Bang, and no complex equations. What we need to know is "In the beginning, God..." This is at once a simple and yet profound statement. It is the statement, through which the rest of scripture is to be interpreted.

2. Without Form and Void

Read Genesis 1:2

Billions of years ago, the universe came into existence in a small point, as a massive primordial atom. This "exploded", and expanded over billions of years, to form the universe we now have.

This is the popular view of how the universe came to be. Readers might recognise this as the Big Bang theory, though, to be fair, it is actually a popularisation of the Big Bang theory, and not quite the same as that believed by modern cosmologists.

The amazing fact is that this popularised, somewhat inaccurate view of how the universe came to be is believed by a majority of Christians today, including those who would claim to be Bible-believing evangelical Christians. There seems today to be a fear of believing what the Bible actually says in Genesis. This is presumably a fear of being made to look ridiculous by people in the world outside our churches. However, the fact that we are addressing this issue at all must be proof that we believe our faith to be a *reasonable* faith, capable of standing up to rigorous scrutiny. The God, who made the universe, and caused its scientific laws to happen, is not suddenly going to be fooled by a scientific law that He hadn't considered. If we believe Genesis to be true, then we can expect science to confirm this, so long as science is sufficiently up to date.

Let us be clear on this last point. We believe the Bible because it is the word of God. We don't believe it, merely because of being convinced by the science. Nor do we disbelieve it if some science seems to be opposed to the Bible. Time and again, it has been shown that, when better science is available, this verifies God's word. God's word is the standard, by which we judge all other academic pursuits. We can confidently use the Bible in this way, knowing that it will not let us down.

A scientist convinced by the Progressive Creationist view that God created progressively over millions of years, said that it would have taken millions of years for the universe to cool down enough for God to make the Earth. But that view is rather putting the cart before the horse. It presupposes that the universe was created in Big Bang like conditions, thus needing to cool down.

The Bible says that "The Earth was without form, and void".(Genesis 1:2). This suggests that the material required to produce the Earth had been created, but God ad not yet put any form to it. This would suggest that the universe was made at zero energy, and would not require cooling. The opposite would seem to be true. This matter requires some form of warming up. There needs to be an energy input. That energy input seems to be provided by the second half of verse 2: "And the Spirit of God was hovering over the face of the waters".

Before we leave this verse, we should tackle the issue of God making the world without form and void. There are many Christians, concerned by the apparent scientific evidence for millions of years, who propose that there must be a gap of millions of years between Genesis 1:1 and Genesis 1:2. To such Christians, verse 2 should be translated "The Earth *became* without form, and void." This is the well-known Gap Theory.

Gap Theorists suggest that, during the millions of years between these two verses, dinosaurs and other extinct creatures could have existed. Some even propose a race of pre-adamic hominids, without souls, in this era. During this era, Lucifer was to be in control. The story goes that Lucifer's rebellion, as described in Isaiah 14 and Ezekiel 28 could have happened in this period. God then destroyed this ancient world, in a great flood (hence the "waters" and "the deep" of Gen 1), which would account for much of the fossil record. God then had to re-create the Earth, and that is what Genesis 1 is all about. In support of this theory, Gap Theorists quote Is 14 and Ez 28, as stated. They also quote God being described as "The Ancient of Days", for example in Daniel 7:9. Also, Gen 1:28, where God tells man to "Fill the Earth". In the Authorised Version, this reads "Replenish the Earth".

A plain reading of Genesis 1 does not seem to suggest the Gap Theory. The prime motivator for believing the Gap Theory is the belief in millions of years. For a full and detailed criticism of all aspects of the Gap Theory, I recommend you look at Fields' masterly work on the subject.[1] For now, I would like to answer briefly the points made in the

---

[1] Fields, W.W. *Unformed and Unfilled,* A Critique of the Gap Theory, (Burgener Enterprises, 1976)

paragraph above.

When the AV was translated, the word replenish meant only to fill, not to fill again. That is why every English translation other than the AV uses "Fill the Earth" for Gen 1:28, so that removes its use. Also, an argument that God is the Ancient of Days and so disproves Young Earth Creationism is not valid. The phrase Young Earth Creationism is only referring to a comparison with the millions of years that evolutionists want. In fact, six thousand years seems pretty ancient to me, and God was there before that anyway.

As for Is 14 and Ez 28 – whether these passages refer to the fall of Lucifer is open to debate. But one thing is certain: that event could not have happened prior to Day 6 of creation, because "God saw everything that He had made, and indeed it was very good." (Gen 1:31). How could the earth have been very good, if Satan had already become evil? This is also the principle reason for not accepting Lucifer's Flood. How could the earth have been very good, if beneath Adam's feet were the results of death and disease – remembering that death entered the world as a result of Adam's sin. Moreover, as Ken Ham has said, why do we need a Flood that the Bible doesn't talk about to explain the fossil record, when it can be better explained by a flood that the Bible does talk about.

"And darkness was on the face of the deep."

I went to Moldova recently. A team from my church spent a week working with a large Pentecostal Church in the North of Moldova. While we were there, another member of the church was driving a lorry across Europe, packed with humanitarian aid. The story of this lorry journey and our time in Moldova is worth another book in its own right. On the night that the lorry was to arrive, we were all out on the streets of the village, scanning the horizon for signs of the lorry. It was 7pm, but it was pitch black. The village had no street lights. In the UK, we are so used to light pollution in our towns and cities that we forget what the absence of light really means.

In the beginning was complete dark. God does not need light, because He is light. When the New Jerusalem comes, we read "The city had no need of the sun or of the moon to shine in it, for the glory of God illuminated it. The Lamb is its light." (Revelation 21:23). For that reason, some passages in the Bible refer to God as dwelling in darkness.

This is the darkness experienced by Abraham, as he came into the near presence of God. "Now when the sun was going down, a deep sleep fell upon Abram; and behold, horror and great darkness fell upon him." (Genesis 15:12). Some versions translate this as thick darkness. It is a darkness that can be *felt*. The word horror is probably the best word, but it doesn't carry quite the meaning of a Gothic Horror movie. The NIV translates the phrase as "a thick and dreadful darkness". The presence of God is no laughing matter. Even for us who are saved, and know that He loves us as our Father, it is still an awesome matter to be in the presence of God.

This is the same darkness experienced in Egypt at the time of the Exodus. "Then the LORD said to Moses, 'Stretch out your hand toward heaven, that there may be darkness over the land of Egypt, darkness which may even be felt.'" (Exodus 10:21).

This dreadful darkness, then, is indicative of the close presence of God. Someone has said that it is not an evil darkness, rather it is the darkness experienced when a bright light is shone into your eyes. And this darkness was on the face of the deep. Whatever the material that God was using, out of which to fashion the universe, it was clearly deep. Humphreys has suggested that "the deep" was a large sphere of water, at least two light years in diameter.[2] Humphreys has developed a cosmology that fits with current cosmological mathematics as well as a six-day creation, but it will be more appropriate to explain this when we reach Day 4. Suffice to say that his cosmology influences much of what I have to say on these early verses. Further evidence of the original matter being water, is in the third phrase of the verse:

"And the Spirit of God was hovering over the face of the waters."

We have seen above that the *waters* cannot refer to the remnants of a pre-adamic Flood, so it would appear to be referring to the building material of the universe. What is interesting to note at this point, is that the Spirit of God was hovering. God is the source of energy as well as matter. This we must expect, as we are now used to the equation linking mass and energy, even if it is not always fully understood.

---

[2] D.R. Humphreys, *Starlight and Time,* Solving the Puzzle of Distant Starlight in a Young Universe, (Master Books, 1994), p32

3. Day One – Light and Darkness

Read Genesis 1:3 – 5

There are three significant issues to address in the remainder of Day 1.

- The creation of light
- Separation of light from darkness
- The length of the day

We are going to have to tackle the controversial issue of how long the days were at some time, so we may as well tackle it now.

It will not have escaped your notice that this book is called "Just Six Days". The conclusion I have reached, therefore, is that the days of creation are six literal twenty-four hour periods of time.

There are a number of arguments rehearsed against this view. Let's start with the weakest argument.

The most frequent response I get, when I say that the universe was made in six days, is, "Ah, but a day is like a thousand years." This is a quote from the Bible. It is 2 Peter 3: 8. "But, beloved, do not forget this one thing, that with the Lord one day is as a thousand years, and a thousand years as one day." The first thing you will notice is that our Day-Agers have not quoted the whole verse. The second half of the verse more or less cancels out the first half of the verse. The second point to notice is that Peter says that this issue is "one thing". He is making one point, not two. The only way of understanding this seems to be that Peter is saying that time is immaterial to God. He can do a thousand years worth of work in one day, yet a real thousand years seems to be only a day to Him. The third point to note is the context of the verse. It is never right to quote a verse out of context. Verses 7 and 9 clearly give us the context. Here are all three verses.

7 But the heavens and the earth which are now preserved by the same

word, are reserved for fire until the day of judgment and perdition of ungodly men.

8 ¶ But, beloved, do not forget this one thing, that with the Lord one day is as a thousand years, and a thousand years as one day.

9 ¶ The Lord is not slack concerning His promise, as some count slackness, but is longsuffering toward us, not willing that any should perish but that all should come to repentance.

Verse 7 shows us that the passage is not even talking about creation. It is talking about the Second Coming of Jesus. The passage is addressing those people who believe that the fact that Jesus has not returned yet proves that He is not going to return. This is nonsense, says Peter. "The Lord is not slack concerning His promise...", he says. The fact that he tarries is a mark of his grace and love.

A fourth point on the phrase "a day is like a thousand years" is that Peter's letter is written in Greek, whereas Genesis is written in Hebrew. The Greek word for *day* does not necessarily help us with a definition for the Hebrew word for *day*.

A fifth and final point concerns Psalm 90:4 "For a thousand years in Your sight Are like yesterday when it is past". A very learned pastor in my church said "If all time is as yesterday, future time will not get very far, for if all time is as yesterday, it has not even started."[1]

With the greatest of respect, I have to say that the clichéd reaction of answering the problem of six-day creation with "A day is like a thousand years" is rather lazy thinking.

This brings us to ask why people want to convince themselves that the days are not real 24 hour days. A longer, uncertain length of day appeals to two types of Christians: Theistic Evolutionists and Progressive Creationists.

Theistic Evolutionists want to believe in God **and** evolution. They would say that God created *through* evolution. "God could have created through evolution, if he wanted to, couldn't he?" What do I answer to this? Of course, God could have done anything. He could have reversed all the scientific laws that render evolution impossible, and caused it to happen, but the fact is that He didn't. If He had created us by evolution, then I would venture to say that the Bible would be written that way. The

---

[1] I owe these thoughts to Pastor Owen Dando

Bible, after all, contains many startling passages that run counter to the supposed primitive beliefs of the time. For example, Isaiah says of God: "It is He who sits above the circle of the earth" (Is 40:22). We might as well say that God could have given us the Nine Commandments. After all, I have difficulty with that tenth one about coveting. But that is not how God did it – instead He gave us the Ten Commandments.

Progressive Creationists and Day-Age creationists are not convinced by the theory of evolution. Like us, they oppose Darwinism, but they accept the geological age of the earth, as measured by evolutionary science. This they use to explain the fossil record. Progressive Creationists also believe the universe itself unfolded slowly, but we have dealt with that issue in chapter 1.

The theological problem that all these views have is that they put the fossil record before Adam's sin. Yet the Bible makes clear that death came into the world as a result of sin. "Nevertheless death reigned from Adam to Moses, even over those who had not sinned according to the likeness of the transgression of Adam, who is a type of Him who was to come." (Romans 5:14). The effect of the curse was to be felt by the **whole** of creation. "Cursed is the ground for your sake; In toil you shall eat of it All the days of your life. Both thorns and thistles it shall bring forth for you" (Genesis 3:17, 18). "For the creation was subjected to futility, not willingly, but because of Him who subjected it in hope; because the creation itself also will be delivered from the bondage of corruption into the glorious liberty of the children of God." (Romans 8:20, 21). If there was death and disease in the world before Adam sinned, then what was the curse all about? And how could God look at a world containing such death and disease and say "indeed it was very good" (Genesis 1:31)?

The issue of whether the Hebrew word *yom* means *day*, or not, only seems to arise in Genesis 1. For example, consider a Bible study on Joshua 6:3, 4.

"You shall march around the city, all you men of war; you shall go all around the city once. This you shall do six days. And seven priests shall bear seven trumpets of rams' horns before the ark. But the seventh day you shall march around the city seven times and the priests shall blow the trumpets."

17

Now, imagine how the Bible discussion group could go. Remember, a day is like a thousand years, so maybe Joshua marched his men round the city of Jericho once every thousand years. He did this six times. Six thousand years later, he took another thousand years to march around seven times.

Why would no one in their right mind interpret Joshua in this way? Dr. John Morris has this to say about the Hebrew word *yom*.

> It occurs over 2000 times in the Old Testament, and it almost always certainly means a solar day, and always could mean a solar day. But, when uncertainty arises, the Bible must be used to interpret itself, most specifically the context of the word, other usages of the word, and other passages on the same subject.[2]

Morris goes on to show that, whereas *yom* usually means *day* outside Genesis 1, it always means *day*, if it is attached to time of day concepts, such as evening or morning, or if it is counted. In Genesis 1, every day is listed by number (first day, second day etc.) and evening and morning are mentioned. It is a bit of a clue, isn't it? The truth is that in Genesis 1, the word day means day, means 24 hour period. Any other translation does no justice to the context.

Let us examine a final theological point. I often wondered why God didn't just create the universe instantly. As omnipotent God, He would have had no difficulty. The answer is found in the Ten Commandments.

> Remember the Sabbath day, to keep it holy. Six days you shall labour and do all your work, but the seventh day is the Sabbath of the LORD your God. (Exodus 20:8-10).

God set the pattern of creation in a week, for our benefit. The week is the only one of our timescales that has no astronomical basis. The day is due to the rotation of the Earth. The year is the period of the Earth's orbit. The month approximates to the orbit of the Moon. But the week has no astronomical basis. It is God's time period, and it is man's time period, created for us, because it is ideally suited to our needs. Attempts to create longer or shorter weeks have failed. But if the universe were not

[2] Morris, J.D., *The Young Earth,* (Master Books)

really created in six days, then God's reasoning on why we should keep the Sabbath holy is flawed. In fact, God set the weekly pattern of work, rest and worship at the beginning of time itself. If we say otherwise, we undermine the moral authority of the Ten Commandments. After all, if the reasoning behind one of the commandments is flawed, why not all the rest as well?

Having decided that the week is a non-astronomical unit, we can say that the day most definitely is an astronomical unit. The day is caused by the rotation of the earth on its axis. It thus requires periods of light and darkness, and a rotation of the planet. It follows that in Genesis 1:3-5, we are witnessing God setting the Earth spinning. In order to define day and night, we require light. So we read that God made light. Night occurs currently on the hemisphere of the earth pointing away from the Sun. It follows that on Day 1, there must have been a point source of light. Yet the Sun itself was not made until Day 4.

There is nothing strange in all this. It is only because we have been, as Ken Ham puts it, evolutionised, that we feel we cannot talk about light and day and night without reference to the Sun. But in order for the day to be defined, all we need is light, and a separation of light and darkness. That separation is caused by the Earth itself.

We have already seen that the energy of the universe was contributed by the Spirit of God hovering over the waters. High School students learn that there are nine different forms of energy (heat, light, kinetic, elastic potential, gravitational potential, chemical, sound, electrical and nuclear). A-level students then find that, in fact, there are only two types – kinetic and potential. All other forms of energy are just instances of these two.

Light incorporates both kinetic and potential energy. There is a movement of electromagnetic fields. This movement, by simple harmonic motion, is against the electromagnetic forces, thus causing a difference in potential against these forces. When the potential is greatest, the movement is momentarily at rest; i.e. the crest or trough of the wave. This rippling motion of the universe's electromagnetic waves themselves seems to be exactly the sort of energy that would be directly provided by the Spirit hovering. In his work mentioned earlier, Humphreys proposes[3] that the Spirit Himself became the localised source

---

[3] *ob cit*

of light. This is not to say that the Holy Spirit is localised, otherwise He couldn't dwell in all of us simultaneously, but that He chose to be the local source of light energy at creation. He was to be that source, until Day 4, when a new object, the Sun, was made to be our material source of light.

This analysis demonstrates to us how special we are. I am often asked, is there life on other planets. I strongly suspect that the answer is no, because the Genesis account is remarkably geocentric and anthropocentric. This is not to say that the Earth is at the centre of the universe – the Earth's orbit is easiest to understand if we assume it is orbiting the Sun. But the central place in Genesis is given to the Earth, and the central character in Genesis is Adam, and the human race in general.

4. Day Two – The Heavens

Read Genesis 1: 6 – 8

The understanding of the events of Day Two hinge on what the word *firmament* means.

The word firmament was introduced to the English language from the Latin Vulgate. The Vulgate was a Latin translation of the Bible. In the Vulgate, verse 6 reads *"dixit quoque Deus fiat firmamentum in medio aquarum et dividat aquas ab aquis"* This in turn is largely written in Latin from the Greek. Now the Old Testament was not written in Greek, but in Hebrew. However, a Greek translation was prepared in Alexandria between about 280 and 200BC. The Septuagint is usually abbreviated as LXX. In the LXX, verse 6 reads "και ειπεν ο θεος γενηθητω στερεωμα εν μεσω του υδατος και εστω διαχωριζον ανα μεσον υδατος και υδατος και εγενετο ουτως". The word for firmament is στερεωμα (*stereoma*), but in fact, this means expanse. The Latin *firmamentum* has the same connotations, so the original emphasis in our English Bibles was one of expanse. It will be seen that this is the word, from which we get our prefix stereo, as in stereophonic. The idea is that there is an expansive sound, not just produced by two speakers. Modern stereo systems for example often have 4 or 5 speakers of different types. In the Hebrew, the word is *raki'a*, which gives an impression of stretching out, in the same way as a blacksmith hammers metal, or a baker rolls pastry.

The word is used a few times in Genesis 1. "And God called the firmament Heaven." (v8). From this verse, we see that the word firmament is going to be interchangeable with the word heaven. This is emphasized by what God says in v14. "Then God said, 'Let there be lights in the firmament of the heavens...'". In verses 14, 15 and 17, both firmament and heavens are being used to describe the sky. In verse 20, however, the word describes atmosphere.

In Psalm 19:1, the combination of heavens and firmament seems to describe the entire universe. "The heavens declare the glory of God; And the firmament shows His handiwork." This would seem to fit with what is said in verse 14 about the stars. It allows for these objects to be placed *in* the firmament. Some have assumed, falsely, that this talk of the firmament is unscientific, or refers to some earlier belief in celestial orbs and spheres. In fact, the concept of the firmament fits with modern notions of Physics and Astronomy.

Psalm 150 exhorts us to "Praise the LORD! Praise God in His sanctuary; Praise Him in His mighty firmament!", though in the NIV, this says "Praise the LORD. Praise God in his sanctuary; praise him in his mighty heavens." Similar comparisons of language usage can be made in Ezek. 1:22, 10:1, and Dan. 12:3.

It would appear that the word for firmament can have the following meanings, depending on the context, and sometimes a mixture of these meanings: expanse, sky, air, atmosphere, space, universe, heaven, heavens.

There is a second element, in verses 6 to 8, which we must investigate. It is the waters. The Hebrew word used is plural. In such a context it seems to imply a gathering of water quantity in one place, such as the waters of an ocean, as in Psalm 18:15: "Then the channels of the sea were seen". In these Genesis verses, we assume that the waters were all gathered into one place. We are still talking about the formation of the universe, however. So is this passage referring to water on the surface of the Earth, or elsewhere?

We cannot make a definitive answer, but we can suggest models that might help us to understand. These models are not to be taken as "gospel". If evidence shows them to be wrong, it will not destroy our belief in the truth of Genesis. It would appear, however, that whatever model we adopt, the dominant material on days 1 and 2 was water.

The traditional creationist view, which has stood us in good stead for four decades, is that the firmament is the atmosphere. Thus the waters above the firmament constitute a water vapour canopy above the atmosphere. Morris, in that great commentary of his on Genesis, which has been so helpful to many of us for so long, says:

> The "waters above the firmament" thus probably constituted a vast blanket of water vapour above the troposphere and probably above the stratosphere as well, in the high-temperature region now known as the ionosphere, and extending far into space. They could not have been the clouds of water droplets which now float in the atmosphere, because the scripture says they

were "above the firmament." Furthermore, there was no "rain upon the earth" in those days (Gen. 2:5), nor any "bow in the cloud" (Gen 9:13), both of which must have been present if these upper waters represented merely the regime of clouds which functions in the present hydrologic economy.[1]

Time has moved on since the Genesis Record. Morris is rightly showing that the waters above the firmament could not have been clouds. But in doing so, he argues that the firmament is the atmosphere. The stars would thus be outside this firmament, whereas later verses suggest that the stars are *in* the firmament.

I prefer Russell Humphreys' cosmology[2] at this point. I will give a fuller account of Humphreys' cosmology in the discussions of Day 4, as it is more appropriate at that point. But on the current verses, Humphreys' Cosmology suggests that "the deep" was a sphere of water at least two light-years in diameter. In Day 2, this sphere is split, suggests Humphreys, by the energy of the Holy Spirit. In this way, Humphreys is trying to explain the expansion of space itself, as well as any constituent parts thereof. He has postulated that God began the universe as a black hole, changing it to a white hole at this point in day 2. As will be seen later, the black hole/white hole concept is used, with relativity theory, to explain the size of the universe and the distances light travels, while still accounting for six days of creation about 6000 years ago.

By direct intervention God begins stretching out space, causing the ball of matter to expand rapidly, thus changing the black hole to a white hole. He marks off a large volume, the "expanse" ("firmament" in the KJV) within the deep, wherein material is allowed to pull apart the fragments and clusters as it expands, but He requires the "waters below" and the waters above" the expanse to stay coherently together.[3]

In this model, space itself is inside the waters above the firmament. There is therefore a boundary to the physical universe. This latter point is fundamental to Humphreys' arguments on the positioning of the stars, but if we continue to pursue his model for the moment, it helps explain

---

[1] Morris, H.M., *The Genesis Record*, (Baker Book House, 1976), p59

[2] Humphreys, D.R., *Starlight and Time*, (Master Books, 1994)

[3] Humphreys, p35

unusual concepts such as Paul's visit to the Third Heaven.

This analysis enables the positioning of the stars in Heaven – i.e. in the expanse of space produced on Day 2.

The idea of a bounded universe resonates with other parts of scripture.

> Where were you when I laid the foundations of the earth? Tell Me, if you have understanding. Who determined its measurements? Surely you know! Or who stretched the line upon it? To what were its foundations fastened? Or who laid its cornerstone, When the morning stars sang together, And all the sons of God shouted for joy? (Job 38:4-7)

> Bless the LORD, O my soul! O LORD my God, You are very great: You are clothed with honour and majesty, Who cover Yourself with light as with a garment, Who stretch out the heavens like a curtain. (Psalm 104:1,2)

This whole process gives an impression of a God who is active and at work. We see here God putting into place the physical laws that we observe throughout the universe.

So with this preparation of the expanse of the universe, God closes Day 2, and prepares the way for His work on the surface of the Earth itself.

5.   Day Three – Land and Plants

Read Genesis 1: 9 – 13

Day three witnesses two important aspects to creation. The first is the separation of water and land. The second is the creation of plant life.

Having seen the separation of waters above and below the firmament, we now see the gathering of the waters under the firmament into one place, and the appearance of dry land. We are clearly now looking at the geological make up of the antediluvian world.

As with the account on the first two days, we need to note the economy of God's creativity. We read "And God said..." then we read "and it was so." From the beginning of creation, it has been the case that the word of God is not to be thwarted. God's word is complete, authoritative and inerrant. What God says, happens.

In this case, we note that God gathers the waters into one place. This would seem to suggest that there was only one ocean and one continent. Suddenly, we are on familiar territory. We are used to the concept of an early, single continent, because it is what evolutionary scientists also believe. It is sometimes wrongly assumed that creationists are trying to undermine everything that scientists say. That is not so. The scientific facts for creationists are exactly the same as the scientific facts for evolutionists. It is simply our interpretations of those facts that are different. So we use the same evidence. The "jigsaw" model of the Earth's continents seems to make a lot of sense. It is well known that the continent of South America, for example, seems to fit against the coast of Africa, and the East and West coasts of the Atlantic Ocean appear to be parallel. Where we differ from the evolutionists is the timescale, during which this all happened.

The idea of a single antediluvian continent is important for other reasons. When Noah built the Ark, the offer of salvation on the Ark was open to anyone. As it happens, it was only taken by Noah, his three sons and all their wives, eight people in all, but the offer was there for all who would repent. Hebrews 11:7 states that Noah condemned the world by his Ark. This would not have been possible, if it was clearly impossible for some humans to reach the Ark. The extraordinary length of time that it took to build the Ark, coupled with Noah's preaching, suggest that it was theoretically possible for all to reach the Ark. Although full discussion of the meaning of the Ark is best discussed elsewhere, one more factor is worth consideration. The Ark was filled by at least one pair of every kind of land animal and bird. In order for these to make it to the Ark, they had to be able to journey over land.

Incidentally, a discussion of land animals also suggests that the immediate postdiluvian world was also one continent, explaining the spread of animals to all parts of the globe. The division of this one continent could then be placed in Genesis 10 – the days of Peleg, when the Earth was divided.

To return to our current chapter, we read, for the first time, in verse 10 "And God saw that it was good". This is not to say that the Earth or universe was evil on Days one and two. If it were, as some would suppose, God could not now say that everything is now good. But something can be not evil, yet not good. Such a thing might be incomplete. Even now, God's creation is not complete, but at Day 3 He had made a planet ready for bearing life. He had a hydrological cycle in place, and He had some dry land, on which to start to place plants and animals. That was something to make God pause and look around and declare it to be good, even though it is not yet fully finished.

But God had not finished His programme of creativity for Day Three. Next, He sets to work on plant life. The description of His work points to three lessons.

One. The description of grass, herbs and trees would appear to be an all encompassing phrase referring to all types of plant life. So all of it came into existence at this point.

Two. The plants were created with all their organ systems already in place and working. We are told that the plants were created ready to bear seeds and fruit, even before insects were created to cause pollination. This is not to imply that insect pollinated plants could produce seed in any other way – after all, they only had a couple of days to wait. It does, however, imply that all systems were in place at the beginning, and did not have to evolve.

Three. We are introduced to the word *kind*. All the plants were created able to reproduce "according to its kind". This is the first appearance of the word *kind*, and we need to understand its significance, and the reason why I keep italicising it. The Hebrew word is *min* and it is being used in a specific way in Genesis. It is to be understood scientifically in a specific way. The Biblical *kind* is not the same as the word *species*. Species is an observable study that is in constant flux – a species being a type of plant or animal, isolated from others, incapable of interbreeding (usually) with members of other species. The development of species has long been used as a rod to beat creationists with. The Paper Tiger argument adopted by evolutionists is that creationists believe in the fixidity of species. We do not. Species are clearly observed to develop. The infamous Darwin's Finches would be an example that in fact, creationists have no problem with. You see, although the finches clearly adapt and develop, they remain at all times finches. This is not evolution, and there will be more discussion on this, when we look at the creation of animals.

Because of this, creationist scientists have now proposed the use of a new word, which is actually a transliteration of the Hebrew. The word is **baramin**, from the Hebrew for *created kind*, and sums up what we now believe about these kinds. Using this new word, we can translate verse 12 as "the herb that yields seed according to its *baramin*". The word baramin is thus wider than species, and has a created element to it. Organisms in different baramins will be unable to interbreed or cross-fertilize in any way. If we later find that such organisms do cross-fertilise, this will then prove an error of classification only, indicating that we have classified one or other of the organisms under the wrong baramin. The ability for two species to cross-fertilise indicates that they are part of the same baramin, but the inability to cross-fertilise does not necessarily imply that two organisms are not part of the same baramin.

The classification of organisms into baramins is a whole new branch of biology, invented by creation scientists. It is being rigorously pursued in peer-reviewed journals, to give a respectability and accountability to the science.[1]

In the case of fruiting trees, for example, we are now used to the idea that all apple trees are part of the same genus, *malus*, along with crab apples. Creationists have no problem with this, nor even if roses are part of the same baramin. God need only to have created one example of this

---

[1] Frair, W, *Baraminology—Classification of Created Organisms*, CRSQ Vol 37 No 2 pp82-91 September 2000

baramin, and the others could have developed from it. We are similarly used to the idea that plums, cherries and wild sloes are related, and we could deduce that they are part of the same baramin. In the abstract of his article, Frair says:

> For decades creationists have been using the word "kind," "type," or "group" for their envisioned categories of genetically unrelated organisms including all those formed by the Creator during Creation Week. Within each of these categories the various species, subspecies, and varieties were conceived to have diversified from common ancestral stock. However, until recent years there has not been a serious comprehensive methodology of classification focusing on characterizing each original category, which is separated by genetic gaps from all other categories. Now baraminology... has developed into a fruitful approach to classification within the creation model.[2]

We will examine this whole concept of baraminology in more detail, when we look at the creation of animals.

We should also note at this point that God does not describe the plants as living things. This seems odd to us. We are familiar with the idea of plants being alive.

Scientists describe an organism as being alive if it fulfils the following seven criteria, usefully remembered with the mnemonic **MRS GREN**.

A living organism can undergo these activities:

- Movement
- Respiration
- Sensitivity
- Growth
- Reproduction
- Excretion
- Nutrition

The Bible is not differing with these. After all, it is clear that these plants created on Day Three can do all seven of these tests. But these are modern scientific tests. Genesis makes an eighth test, which is of an

---

[2] *ibid*

entirely different kind. It is more of a *moral* test. Some organisms are said to be *living* in the sense of having a *living spirit*. It is almost impossible to translate the Hebrew word being used for animals later in this chapter. It might be better for us to transliterate again. The word is **nephesh**. We will use this word to describe a higher level of life, as defined in the Bible. There will be more discussion of this, when we look at Days Five and Six, and, indeed, Genesis Chapter 2. What we can observe for now is that plants do not have this nephesh, this *living spirit*. The rules that apply to the death of nephesh creatures do not apply to plants. Indeed, the death of plants is an entirely different matter to the death of nephesh animals, and perhaps shouldn't be referred to as death at all. Such termination of the life of a plant is not a result of the Fall, and must have happened in the garden prior to the fall, as Adam and Eve would need to reap crops and eat them. As we will discuss later, this lack of nephesh is probably applicable to many animals also.

For now, we will conclude Day Three by noting that God, for a second time in one day, observes that what He has made is good.

6. Day Four – The Bible's Astronomy

Read Genesis 1:14 – 19

At the beginning of Day Four, it is worth noting that God's six-day creation is actually in a pattern, with two groups of three days. This pattern shows three days of creating, mostly *ex nihilo*, followed by three days of *filling*. This pattern is set out in the table below.

Creating		Filling	
Day 1	Universe created	Day 4	Universe filled with Sun, moon, stars etc.
Day 2	Expanse of space created. Atmosphere created. Waters above and below firmament separated	Day 5	Atmosphere filled with birds. Waters beneath firmament filled with fish and sea creatures
Day 3	Land and sea separated. Plants created on dry land.	Day 6	Land animals created. Humans created.

It is doubtful whether any major theological point can be drawn from this symmetry, other than to show that it demonstrates the orderliness of God. He is a God of order, who has created the universe, to work within scientific laws. We can deduce these laws, and in the process, we are, in the words of Johannes Kepler, "Thinking God's thoughts after Him."[1]

There are some who have supposed that this symmetry indicates that Genesis 1 is actually a poem with two verses. It can therefore be interpreted poetically, rather than literally.

---

[1] quoted in *Creation Matters*, vol. 4, no. 3, (Creation Research Society, May 1999), p1

There is no justification for this position. The Bible contains much poetry. Read the Psalms, for example. There are also examples of where one style of Biblical literature changes to another. For example, in Habakkuk, we have prophetic literature changing to poetry.

However, Genesis is all written in the same style. If we believe Genesis 1 to be poetic, we have to believe the accounts of Abraham, Isaac, Jacob and Joseph to be poetic, including events, which are verifiable by extra-biblical sources. Because of the stylistic unity of Genesis, if we take the account of Joseph in Egypt to be history, then we must take the account of the Creation to be history, if we are to do justice to the text and hermeneutics.

Verses 14 and 15 describe God making lights in the firmament.

The first thing we should notice is that the lights are made *in the firmament*. Until Humphreys' developed and published his cosmology[2], this whole idea of creating lights in the firmament confused me. My previous analysis of this passage had led me to suppose that the firmament referred to either the atmosphere or the sky. In either case, the idea of stars, Sun and Moon *in* the firmament did not make sense. Now, Humphreys' model of the universe enables us to identify the universe itself as the firmament, and so these lights being made in the firmament is an activity, which makes sense.

The second thing to notice is the *raison d'être* of these lights. Two reasons are given here. The lights are there to mark out the seasons. This one phrase incorporates all the subtlety of the motion of the objects in the universe.

Because stars are so far away, they appear fixed against the sky. Of course, they are not, and over the centuries, there have been slight changes of the position of stars relative to each other. For example,

---

[2] D.R. Humphreys, *Starlight and Time,* Solving the Puzzle of Distant Starlight in a Young Universe, (Master Books, 1994)

in the times of ancient Egypt, the star we now know as Polaris was not the one directly above the North Pole. This position was held by the star Thuban. In the diagram of the constellation Draco[3], two faint starts from the "little dipper" or "little bear", Ursa Minor, are shown at the bottom left. Polaris is also a member of the constellation Ursa Minor.

The Earth's axis is tilted at an angle of 23° to where it might be expected. The position of the Earth's axis might be expected at 90° to the plane of the Earth's orbit. This angle of tilt causes slightly different stars to be seen in the night sky at different times of the year. Because the stars make apparent patterns in the sky, called constellations, which are easily recognisable, the progress of these constellations can be tracked throughout the year. Thus the star patterns mark out the seasons, and this fact has been known since earliest records began

The tilt of 23° is what causes the seasons, as this enables the Northern Hemisphere to be pointed more towards the Sun in summer, and away in winter, and vice versa for the Southern Hemisphere. It has been suggested that the tilt could have been caused by the catastrophic effects of the Flood. I think this unlikely however. It would seem to me that the tilt of 23° has been there from the beginning, as the mention of seasons in verse 14 seems to demand it.

The Sun and the Moon are also timekeepers. The Moon orbits the Earth once every 28 days. It also rotates on its axis once every 28 days. This means that it always keeps the same face towards the Earth. It was not until the Moon probes of the 1960s and 1970s that we began to see the reverse side of the Moon. The reverse side of the Moon is far more rocky and mountainous than the near side, with less of the *mare*. The Moon's *mares* are the large grey coloured areas. They are greyer than the surrounding areas, because they are flat plains, rather than mountainous, and therefore reflect less sunlight to the Earth. The Moon's light is entirely due to reflected sunlight – it has no light of its own. Its 28 day orbit is seen from the Earth in the form of phases, from New Moon, through quarters (crescents and half-moons) to Full Moon and back again. This timescale has also been known since earliest times.

The Sun also gives us timescales. The orbit of the earth around the Sun takes about 365.3 days. This is the length of our year. The Earth's orbit is elliptical, rather than circular. If the Earth's orbit were circular,

---

[3] taken from http://www.astro.uiuc.edu/~kaler/sow/dra-t.html

and the Earth's axis not tilted away from the perpendicular, then we would notice no seasons. The ancient timescales, plotting the year's course by the seasons is entirely astronomical in nature. The Earth's rotation about its own axis takes 24 hours. This is the length of the day. From Day Four onwards, following the creation of the Sun, this rotation causes us to see an apparent motion of the Sun across the sky. We can plot this apparent path of the Sun across the sky. In reality, it is the path of the Earth around the Sun. Thus, in this same region of the sky, we find all the other planets, moving across the sky, relative to the "fixed" stars. These are our near neighbours, the "wandering stars" that orbit the Sun.

This brings us to the second reason that these lights are in the sky. They are there to give light to the Earth.

The Sun is there to rule the day. It does indeed govern the day, as its apparent motion counts off our hours. Thus the sundial can be used as a remarkably accurate clock.

The Moon governs the night. The Moon sometimes appears during the day, but it cannot govern the day. When it appears in daytime, it is pale and difficult to see. But at night, it is seen in its full glory.

When we consider the multiplicity and complexity of the universe, it is startling to find that the creation of the stars is summed up in one phrase – "He made the stars also"! In Psalm 8:3, the stars are described as "the work of your fingers". Psalm 19 gives another reason for the existence of the universe – "The heavens declare the glory of God; And the firmament shows His handiwork." (Ps 19:1).

Notice that the Sun, Moon and *stars* exist to give light to the Earth. But what is it that makes the Sun shine.

Conventional wisdom tells us that the Sun shines by nuclear fusion. Strangely enough, this causes a major problem for scientists. Nuclear fusion should cause the release of vast numbers of neutrinos. Yet neutrino capture on the Earth finds a very small percentage of the expected neutrino bombardment.

An earlier scientific model suggests that the heat and light of the Sun are caused by gravitational collapse of the Sun as a star. Its material is sucked towards the centre, but it is large enough not to show an appreciable change in size (though some experiments seem to show a shrinking Sun). The problem with this theory is that it only accounts for a few million years of solar history. Were the Sun to be more than a few million years old, then gravitational collapse would have caused the Sun to disappear, or become a black hole. But the few million years is more than enough for creationists to accept.

There seems to be no harm in suggesting that the Sun's power comes from a combination of both these factors.

Yet there is something very strange about the light produced by the stars. This strange property of the light of the stars is known as Olber's Paradox.

The Paradox is stated as follows: Why is the sky at night not as uniformly bright as the sun?[4]

This might seem an odd question, but let us analyse the reasons for posing it. Supposing there is an infinite number of stars. Suppose space is infinitely large. And suppose that the distribution of stars throughout the universe is approximately constant. These three assumptions are, in fact, central to the Big Bang Theory of cosmology. If the Sun were twice as far away, its apparent angular diameter would be half the size, therefore its area would be a quarter the size. This apparent "room" could be filled by other stars. If these stars are infinite in number, in an infinite space, then the amount of light shining from every apparent direction in a solid sphere in every direction, as viewed from the Earth. Thus the entire night sky should be bright as day.

This is obviously not the case, so we need to explain why. One explanation is that maybe the number of stars is not infinite, or that maybe the distribution is not even. Both these models are anathema to the evolutionary scientist. Another option is that the universe is younger than people suppose, so not every star's light has reached us yet. This fits with many, though not all, creationist cosmologies. Yet another explanation is that the red shift of receding stars is preventing their light reaching the Earth.

Without plumping for the moment for my preferred answer to Olber's paradox, I want to mention that Olber's paradox is a considerable difficulty for evolutionary theory. Big Bang cosmology suggests an unbounded universe, with no centre. Thus it should be possible to see a star in every possible direction one looks. This would make the night sky light all over.

In fairness, it should be pointed out that Big Bang cosmologists do

---

[4] Several web sites cover this paradox. See for example
http://zebu.uoregon.edu/~imamura/123/lecture-5/olbers.html

address this problem. They point to the evidence (which creationists do not challenge) of red shift amongst stars. Thus the light of many very red-shifted stars does not reach the Earth. So it is not that Big Bang cosmologists have no answer. It is simply that I think one possible creation cosmology has a better answer. I pose the paradox now, because there is actually more than one creationist cosmology, and some of these do not satisfactorily answer Olber's Paradox.

We should now address a problem, for which, until recently, creation scientists did not seem to have an adequate explanation. It is this: how do we reconcile a belief in a 6000 year old Earth and a six-day creation, with the observation that stars can be many, many light years away – sometimes millions of light years.

A light year is not a unit of time. It is a unit of distance. The speed of light in a vacuum is 3×10^8 ms^{-1} (186000 miles per hour!). From these figures, it is possible to calculate that a light year is about 9.5×10^{15}m, which is about 6 million million miles (6,000,000,000,000 miles). A light year is defined, therefore, as the distance light travels in a vacuum in one year.

Space itself is generally accepted as being more or less a vacuum. So we are seeing stars, not as they are now, but as they were when the light left the star. The brightest star in the Northern Hemisphere is Sirius. Sirius is 8 light years away. I am writing this book in early 2004. The light from Sirius that I observed last night began its journey in 1996.

Our problem is that, if a distant galaxy is a million light years away, then its light began a million years ago, yet we believe the world to be only 6000 years old. Those who want to believe in millions of years, especially Progressive Creationists, have used this observation to beat Young Earth Creationists with.

Distances of stars can be measured. There may be some doubt about the accuracy of some of the measurement methods, but not enough to undermine the possibility of millions of light years. For example, a Big Bang cosmologist might measure a galaxy at 1 million light years away. If his calculations are 50% wrong, that still leaves the galaxy at 500,000 light years away.

A commentary like this is probably not the best place to discuss the various methods of measuring star distances. A number of methods are used, among them being triangulation, Cepheid variables and the red shift of stars. More information on how these methods work can be obtained from more specialised creationist literature, or from Big Bang literature, because we are not disputing the methodologies.[5,6,7]

What we must tackle here is the problem that these measurements cause. There have been a number of possible attempts to reconcile the vast distances with the Young Earth model.

Mature Creation

According to this theory, God created the star's light already on its way to Earth. The argument is that God gave the universe an apparent age. This is compared to the apparent ages of Adam and Eve. We can assume that, because Adam and Eve were able to have children immediately after leaving Eden, that they were created with an apparent age in their twenties, at least. It was only a few days since they were created, yet they were adults.

Where the analogy seems to fall down is that Adam would have no memories of life as a child, because he never was a child, but the universe does have "memories" of time before the 6000 years of creation. We see supernovae in distant galaxies, for example. A supernova is the massive explosion of a star. Are we saying that this event, whose light has taken millions of years to reach us, never actually happened? Are we saying that God invented this event, to fool us? This is like an old belief that God created all the fossils already in the rocks.

I am not saying that God could not have created the universe in such a way. I am saying that I find it an uncomfortable and unconvincing model of the universe. Nevertheless, it is the model of the universe acceptable to many eminent creation scientists. Although I believe that Adam and Eve were created mature, I do not think that the universe was analogously related looking old.

Speed of light decay

Setterfield and Norman have proposed that the speed of light has

---

[5] De Young, D.B., *Astronomy and the Bible*, Baker Books, 2000, p64

[6] Burgess, S., *He Made the Stars Also*, Day One, 2001

[7] http://imagine.gsfc.nasa.gov/YBA/M31-velocity/Doppler-shift-3.html

decayed over the 6000 years of Earth's history.[8] They have analysed historic measurements of the speed of light and plotted these against time. It is their claim that these measurements fit on a curve with the equation

$$\Lambda = a + e^{kt}(b + dt).$$

In this equation, a, b, k and d are constants, t is time, and Λ is the cosmological constant, proportional to c^2; c being the speed of light in a vacuum.

Their work, published on the internet at reference 8, has been extensively peer-reviewed. On the positive side, it seems to offer an explanation of how light from distant stars reaches the earth today. It doesn't seem to explain, however, how light from distant stars reached the Earth on Day Six of creation, when man was created. Is this important?

Setterfield and Norman make a number of predictions on behaviours of other phenomena. Many physics formulae depend on c – for example Planck's Constant, which determines the size of the small packets or *quanta* of energy emitted by excited atoms. (It just means they're hot, OK? It doesn't mean they are jumping for joy!). Planck's Constant is would actually not be constant if the speed of light carried, so atomic spectra would be affected by this. But no observation has yet been made to support this view.

Setterfield's ideas on c-decay got creation scientists working on scientifically valid models of the universe. For that he is to be commended. Unfortunately, his model does not seem to be as exciting as it once appeared, and is now largely rejected by creation scientists.

Riemann Space

Bernhard Riemann (1826–1866) himself is not responsible for this creation model, although he was a creationist. His work was concerned with the theoretical application of non-Euclidean geometries.

---

[8] Setterfield, B. and Norman, T., *The Atomic Constants, Light and Time*, 1987 http://www.setterfield.org/report/report.html

Euclid it was who realised that the three angles of a triangle add up to 180°. Riemann proposed alternative universes, where the angles of a triangle could be less or more than in the Euclidean model. We are so used to geometrical problems from our school Maths days, that we forget that Euclid actually had to base his geometry on a number of assumptions. Euclid based his geometry on 23 definitions, 5 postulates, 5 common notions and 48 propositions. These form his *elements*. Riemann challenged these.

Some creationists have taken Riemann's ideas on curvature of space, and given what they claim to be reasonable assumptions. Using these assumptions they have calculated that light only needs to travel 15.7 light years through curved space, even if the stars are millions of light years away.

Although these calculations are convenient, they involve a number of assumptions, which do not seem fully justified.

Starlight and Time[9]

I have already stated that this is the cosmology that makes most sense to me. To understand the cosmology fully, you need to read Humphreys' book, and maybe watch the animated video of the same name, which is available from Answers in Genesis (www.answersingenesis.org).

A summary of Humphreys' cosmology is in order, however.

In his cosmology, he proposes that God made the universe as a sphere of water, at least 2 light years in diameter. He then uses maths, valid under Riemann equations, and Einstein's Theories of Relativity, in the same sort of way as Stephen Hawkings[10] and other Big Bang cosmologists, with the exception that he changes two assumptions. Big Bang cosmologists assume the universe to be unbounded and without a centre. They also assume matter to be approximately evenly distributed throughout the universe. Humphreys assumes that the universe is bounded. It therefore has a centre. Matter is not uniformly distributed throughout the universe, because there is a region beyond the bound where there is no matter.

It is not usually realised that Big Bang cosmologists believe matter to

---

[9] Humphreys, D. R., *Starlight and Time*, Master Books, 2003
[10] Hawking, S.W., *A Brief History of Time*, Transworld, 1988

be evenly distributed. A popular view of the Big Bang is as an explosion of a primordial atom. In fact, because of curvature of space, Big Bang cosmologists believe that space itself was folded and curved in on itself, so that when there was a primordial small atom, that atom filled the entire universe of the time. Space itself thus expands.

We are familiar with two dimensional analogies of three dimensional space. We often see wire frame diagrams of space. If the universe was created bounded, then it must have a centre. We can assume, then, that the Earth is close to that centre. If there was a centre, there would be gravitational force towards the centre. This would be like a depression in our 2D wire frame. If the Earth were at the bottom of that depression, there would be a horizon beyond which we cannot see.

Many experiments have shown that time actually runs slower under greater gravitational fields. If we were observing from the depth of this depression, then at the *event horizon* time would be whizzing by. A clock's hands would be a blur. Thus, during Day 4 of creation on Earth, millions of years of star formation could take place at and beyond the event horizon. The maths involved to show this are based on the maths for time variation in black holes and white holes.

The water of Day One would collapse under its own gravity, and under the command of God, to form new elements fusion. In Day 2, the waters above and below the firmament are separated, and space itself is expanded by God. Above the firmament is the boundary of the universe – a layer of water. The event horizon would still be beyond this. On day 3 the waters above the firmament pass through the event horizon, and this causes the event horizon to shrink, because there is now less matter inside the horizon. On the morning of Day 4, the event horizon reaches Earth. Thus it is that billions of years of star processes take place in the cosmos, while only one day takes place on Earth. At the evening of the fourth day, the event horizon is inside the Earth, and shrinks to nothing, and we have the universe that we have today.

The beauty of this cosmology is that it explains many observed phenomena. For example, we can use the same red shift theories as the Big Bang cosmologists. But what is very exciting is that this fits with other passages of scripture. The word firmament (raki'a) we have already seen means *stretching*.

He stretches out the north over empty space; He hangs the earth on nothing. (Job 26:7).

I am the LORD, who makes all things, Who stretches out the heavens all alone, Who spreads abroad the earth by Myself (Isaiah 44:24).

I would urge readers to study Humphreys' book listed as reference 9. It should be noted, however, that this is still only a scientific model, albeit a very good model. If Humphreys' model also one day proves invalid, it will not overturn our belief that the Bible is true when it says God made the world in six days.

7. Day Five – Creatures of the Air and Water

Read Genesis 1:20 – 23

On Day Five, God made the first two sorts of animals. He made birds and he made sea creatures. Then He did two things that He didn't do for the plants on Day Three – He blessed them, and gave them a command.

Animals are clearly different in God's eyes to plants. What we are witnessing here in Genesis 1 is the bare bones of a Biblical Biology.

A great many of us are used to an unbiblical biology. This biology tells us that we, as humans, are little more than animals ourselves, as we have come from them. It also tells us that animals and plants have all developed from single cellular organisms, which just emerged into being from some primordial soup.

There are some Christians who want to harmonise evolution with the Bible. They are relieved to find that plants are created before animals. They are also relieved to find that marine animals are created before land animals. Unfortunately, other facts are not so convenient. Chief among these is that birds are created at the same time as sea creatures, *before* land animals. This is highly inconvenient, as birds are supposed to have evolved from land reptiles, such as dinosaurs. God's word does not fit with evolutionary theory on this point, and they cannot both be right. The position of the Christian evolutionists is thus made untenable.

Then God said, "Let the waters abound with an abundance of living creatures" (v20)

God brought forth a lot of marine creatures, all over the ocean, all at once. The repetition of abound/ abundance shows how vast the number of sea creatures was to be. Today we know that there are more species of animal in the depths of the ocean than all the land animals put together. These sea creatures are not just fish, though there are clearly a lot of those. There would also be marine invertebrates and mammals, such as whales and dolphins, and possibly marine reptiles. The latter can be assumed, because the phrase translated in the NKJV as "great sea creatures" is translated as "great whales" in the AV, but the same phrase elsewhere in scripture is often rendered by the AV as "dragons". These, we can surmise, would be the ichthyosaurs and plesiosaurs – maybe the great sea monsters of legend.

And let birds fly above the earth across the face of the firmament of the heavens.

Whereas the first part of the verse refers to a multitude of types of sea creature, only one classification of aerial creature is given – birds. This probably helps to emphasise to us the impossibility of evolution. Birds thus evolved before flying insects, bats or pteradons. They are said to fly across the face of the firmament of the heavens. This indicates that the firmament can sometimes refer to the atmosphere. Not for one moment do we suppose that there were creatures that could fly in space. It is perhaps significant that they do not fly *in* the firmament, but *across the face of* the firmament. The atmosphere can be said to be across the face of the sky. Stars, on the other hand, were placed *in* the firmament.

God gave the birds and marine creatures a blessing. He also commanded them to "be fruitful and multiply, and fill the waters in the seas, and let birds multiply on the earth." The reproductive capacity of animals is thus blessed and defined as *good* by God Himself.

But how can God bless animals? The first thing to note from God's blessing is that animals are not the same as plants. There is a different sort of life. The clue is that they are described as **living creatures**. The Hebrew word is *nephesh*, and is usually translated elsewhere in scripture as *soul*. The concept that we call soul is not restricted to humans. Don't get me wrong. In our studies of Day Six, we will see that there is a considerable difference between humans and other animals. But that difference is not due to soul.

How many people have kept a well-loved pet dog or cat for years, and know its "personality"? I had a ginger cat that I knew well. I swear that it would look at me in a particular way. It was familiar with me. It knew my smell. I knew it, even when I saw other ginger cats.

Christians who mourn the loss of a dead dog, cat, budgie etc. are not being silly or sentimental. There was a bond with the animal. Yes, they knew its life was not as valuable as a human, and they allowed the vet to put the fog down – something they would never do to their Granddad (I hope). Yet the animal had sufficient of a soul to give it personality that was recognisable. We can recognise this as truth, without making silly claims about our pet cat going to heaven.

The situation is more complicated, though, because it would appear that not every type of animal has nephesh. This would certainly make sense if lower invertebrates were not classed as nephesh animals. For example, corals are animals, rather than plants. Yet the phrase *Yam Suph*, used in Exodus of the Red Sea, and sometimes incorrectly translated as "Sea of Reeds" could probably refer to the large coral reefs in the Red Sea. Thus these simple animals are classified with plants, because they lack nephesh.

In that case, we need to know what nephesh is. We have a clue from Leviticus 17:11.

> For the life of the flesh is in the blood, and I have given it to you upon the altar to make atonement for your souls; for it is the blood that makes atonement for the soul.

The life is in the blood. Possibly we are referring to haemoglobin in the blood. Whatever our interpretation, it would appear that we can at least classify all vertebrates, which all have blood as we would understand it, as nephesh creatures. Whether or not we can classify any invertebrates as nephesh is an open question. Certain invertebrates have haemoglobin, and some invertebrates seem to show "personality". Whatever we might say, it seems clear that this would be a fruitful area of study for baraminologists.

Now that we have re-introduced the term *baraminology*, we should note that, in common with the plants, these marine creatures were created "according to their kind". Once again, we might usefully employ the term baramin. Each of the creatures was created according to its baramin.

Frair defines a number of helpful terms, for our understanding of this important new science.[1]

---

[1] Frair, W., *Creation Research Society Quarterly Vol 37 No 2 pp82-91 September 2000*

Holobaramin

This is an entire group believed to be related by common ancestry. The Greek word *holos* meaning whole, as in holistic. A group of related specimens could thus be described as holobaraminic.

Monobaramin

From *mono* meaning one. This defines a group of organisms belonging to the same baramin. A monobaramin could thus be a holobaramin or a portion thereof.

Apobaramin

An apobaramin contains the entirety of at least one holobaramin. There may accidentally be more than one holobaramin in the apobaramin. To say that an organism is part of an apobaramin is to state that the organism is not related to any organism outside the baramin, but we are not sure that the apobaramin in question cannot later be subdivided.

Polybaramin

A group of organisms, to which it is helpful to refer, but which comprises of all or part of more than one holobaramin.

These four terms have been developed to enable researchers to identify and classify organisms. The science is still very young, and a good deal of worthwhile research is possible in this field for both professional and amateur scientists.

8. Day Six – Land Animals and Humans

Read Genesis 1:24 – 31

Day Six sees the creation of land animals and humans.

The creation of land animals follows the same pattern as that of other animals on Day 5. The animals are created within baramins. There is no evidence of evolution here. Indeed the order of creation specifically contradicts creation. Birds are assumed to have evolved from land animals, but birds were created before land animals.

The Bible doesn't need to explicitly refer to dinosaurs at this point, for us to know that dinosaurs are included. Dinosaurs, for the most part, were land animals. Dinosaurs are extinct, but then so are many species of mammals, reptiles, amphibian, fish and birds. It is probable that whole baramins have disappeared from the Earth, but they could not have disappeared before the Flood, because God commanded Noah to take two of every baramin on board the Ark. This must have included dinosaurs. Our popular image of dinosaurs today is that of giant creatures. However, most dinosaurs were a lot smaller.

It would appear that the three classifications of land animals have nothing to do with taxonomic classification. Instead, it is a fairly practical and pragmatic classification, relating to how these animals were to interact with mankind. The three classes are:

- Beasts of the earth
- Cattle
- Creeping things

"Beasts of the earth" probably refers to large wild animals. "Cattle" suggests domesticated animals. The "creeping things" are those lower to the ground, and therefore of less immediate importance to mankind. They probably include a large variety of baramins or kinds. The class probably includes non-nephesh creatures like insects, arthropods etc., but

45

also small reptiles, like lizards, and small mammals, like mice.

Evolutionists would want to classify creatures into predators and prey. Even some old-earth creationists have fallen into this trap, by defining the three classes as cattle, other animals and animals to hunt. There would, however have been no hunting before Adam's fall, in chapter 3.

> And God said, "See, I have given you every herb that yields seed which is on the face of all the earth, and every tree whose fruit yields seed; to you it shall be for food. "Also, to every beast of the earth, to every bird of the air, and to everything that creeps on the earth, in which there is life, I have given every green herb for food"; and it was so. (Genesis 1:29,30)

Before the Fall, Adam and Eve did not eat meat. In fact, mankind was not permitted to eat meat until after the Flood (Genesis 9:3). Whether or not any humans had started to eat meat before the Flood, in contravention of God's law, we are not told.

We are told, however, that all the classes of land animals, and the birds, were designed to eat plants, not meat. In fact, verse 30 says nothing about the cattle class, but these are still today acknowledged to be herbivorous. The term *green herb* refers to all types of plant.

This is a startling declaration. What about lions and tigers and bears, you repeat (with Dorothy from the Wizard of Oz)?

Dealing with bears first. In fact, most types of bear are largely herbivorous. All bears are capable of being herbivorous. The most nearly carnivorous bear – the Polar Bear – lives in an area where only meat can today be eaten. But remember God created according to kinds. Evolutionists and baraminologists agree that bears and pandas, and sloth bears, are part of the same kind. Many of these, such as the Giant Panda, are completely herbivorous. The sharp teeth of pandas seem to be remarkably well designed for tearing bamboo, yet evolutionists tell us that they evolved to eat meat.

Lions and tigers are, of course, part of the same baramin. God did not need to create both separately. They almost certainly developed from a common ancestor. Although today's big cats are carnivorous, there is no reason to suppose that their digestive systems could not have been different before the Fall.

Tyrannosaurus had large, sharp teeth. Evolutionists say that this proves he was developed carnivorous. In fact, all it tells us is that it has sharp teeth.

The world's largest bat is the Flying Fox. This creature has large, sharp teeth. They are ideal for ripping through the flesh... of fruit. The Flying Fox lives entirely off fruit.

Even evolutionists have now decided that maybe old T Rex wasn't quite as seen in the film Jurassic Park. Maybe he was a hyena-like scavenger, instead of a tiger like predator.[1] We can accept that, because it could be the post-Fall behaviour of the animal.

This discussion points out an important lesson in the subject of what is science and what is not. Science is about the observations made. Scientific hypotheses are designed to fit the facts and explain them. Hypotheses are capable of scientific testing. But when we place unprovable conjectures onto scientific observation we move beyond science. To say Tyrannosaurus had sharp teeth is one thing. To say how he used those teeth is another.

It should be noted in passing that marine animals are not included in this injunction to eat only green herbs. Certain marine animals would have had no other sort of food. Baleen whales, for example, sieve plankton through what passes for teeth in their mouths. However, we can understand this pre-fall death of small marine animals, because they would presumably have been non-nephesh animals. (It can also be noted that Berndt is of the opinion that the pre-Fall death of nephesh marine creatures is possible[2])

After God had made the land animals, He allowed Himself time to reflect, and He saw that it was all good. This is despite the fact that He hadn't finished His sixth day of creation. But the universe was now good, because everything was in place for the creation of man.

The creation of man and woman is expanded in Genesis chapter 2. For now we will note a few important principles.

The Trinity was involved in Man's Creation.

Then God said, "Let **Us** make man". Man was created by the Word of

---

[1] see http://www.ucmp.berkeley.edu/trex/specialtrex2.html

[2] Berndt, Chard, *The Pre-Fall Mortality of Aquatic Autotrophs and Other Designated Nephesh kinds*, CRSQ Vol 40 No 2 pp85-89 September 2003

God. As we understand from the beginning of John's Gospel, Jesus Christ is the Word of God. Colossians 2:9, 10 says "For in Him dwells all the fullness of the Godhead bodily; and you are complete in Him, who is the head of all principality and power." The whole Trinity is involved in the direct creation of mankind; Father, Son and Spirit. We have an indication of this, by God referring to Himself in the plural – "Let **Us** make man."

Mankind was made in the Image of God

This is what sets man above the animals. Some Christians believe that it is the soul that sets man apart. This cannot be, because as we have seen, the nephesh animals have a soul too, though it may be of a different sort. What sets man apart is that he was created in the image of God.

Mankind is special. We find in chapter 2 that man was not created *ex nihilo*, as the animals were. Instead, Adam was created specially from dust, whereas Eve was created from Adam's side. God was intimately involved in the creation of man.

This is why people understand right and wrong within them. Why do atheists talk about right and wrong? On what basis can they deduce that something is right or wrong?

When I began my Masters course, my tutor was a well known medical ethicist. It was his job to create a new set of ethics. These ethics were built up, like a mathematical set of axioms, from assumptions that had no basis in the Bible. The subjects that we discussed were to do with right and wrong. The essay title that I was assigned was "Sexism and Racism: a false analogy". Without going into the substance of any of the arguments for and against this proposal, the assumption was that sexism and racism are both bad things. The difficulty was in deciding why we considered them to be bad things. Sexism I will deal with shortly, but, briefly, I am opposed to racism and racist attitudes, because I see that we were all descended from the one ancestor, Adam. We are thus all of one blood, as the Apostle Paul put it.

> He has made from one blood every nation of men to dwell on all the face of the earth, and has determined their preappointed times and the boundaries of their dwellings. (Acts 17:26)

48

I find it difficult to see what evolutionary response there can be to racism. It must be said that the vast majority of evolutionists are not racist, and are as horrified by racism as I am. Nevertheless, racist groups have often appealed, with a fair degree of logic, to evolutionary principles, to support their abhorrent views. Ken Ham has written on this subject at length, in his book, "One Blood".[3]

It is the image of God that gives us our sense of right and wrong. The devil's lies are always most powerful when they are half-truths, so the devil was partly right when he told Eve "God knows that in the day you eat of it (the fruit) your eyes will be opened, and you will be like God, knowing good and evil." (Genesis 3:5). It is an aspect of God's nature that He is completely good, and anything less than His perfection is evil. We have that knowledge of good and evil, and it is an aspect of our being created in the image of God. The devil's lie was to imply that to truly know good and evil we have to experience it.

Because of Adam's sin, the image of God within us is tarnished. Note the startling contrast between Genesis 5:1 and 5:3.

In the day that God created man, He made him in the likeness of God.

And Adam lived one hundred and thirty years, and begot a son in his own likeness, after his image, and named him Seth.

Seth, who Eve rightly prophesied was to be the carrier of the promised seed, was begotten in the image of Adam, whereas Adam was created in the image of God. To labour the point a moment, Seth was born in the image of a man who was in the image of God.

The fullness of the image of God was not to be seen again in mankind, until the birth of Jesus, the Last Adam. I have discussed the comparison between Jesus and Adam elsewhere.[4] For now, it is interesting to note that Jesus could be perfect, and still be perfectly human. This is because there was a model of perfect humanity in Adam. If we don't believe in a literal Adam, created perfectly in the image of God, and our failed representative in the garden, then how can we accept

---

[3] Ham, Ken, *One Blood: The Biblical Answer to Racism,* Master Books: 2000

[4] Taylor, P., *Two Men Called Adam*, Just Six Days Publications: 2003

Jesus as human? He becomes some sort of super-human. But the basis of our theology of Jesus being able to save us, is that He was, and is, at once both God and man. The Apostle Paul says:

He is the image of the invisible God, the firstborn over all creation.

There is a strong sense, in which the image of God is restored in our lives, when we come to know Jesus. The image of God is visible in everyone, albeit a tarnished vision. That is why atheists know the difference between right and wrong. That is why there are many good people outside the church, who do many good things. But when the Holy Spirit dwells within us, we have a deeper sense of morality. We still fail. We still make great mistakes. But we know the One from whom all measurement of morality is made.

Mankind was created Male and Female

There are differences between men and women. These differences became more noticeable after the Fall. But this first passage about the creation of men and women in Genesis 1 points out the important similarities.

It should be first noted that Genesis 2 is simply an expansion of this account of the creation of Adam and Eve. There is significance in the fact that Adam and Eve were created differently. But in chapter 1, we are concerned only with the species of mankind as a whole.

Some say it is not politically correct to refer to the human race as mankind. Therefore, some propose new translations of the Bible, which render such phrases as "people". That misses the point. The Bible refers to God with a masculine pronoun. Mankind is made in the image of God, so the Bible is referring to mankind, collectively, in the masculine. One gender had to be chosen. So references to man in this sense are to be taken as references to men and women – humankind. Thus, any promises made to man are in fact made to all people. It was indeed Adam who was the representative in the garden of the entire human race, men and women.

Genesis 1:27 puts it succinctly.

So God created man in His own image; in the image of God He created him; male and female He created them.

Mankind is collectively made in the image of God. He was made male and female. God created *them*.

This means that Jesus is the Saviour of all people – men and women. We have One Lord, One Saviour, One God.

God blessed us

Of course, God blessed animals too. Nevertheless, men and women have a special place in His heart. He made this whole universe for us. We are the culmination of His creation, made for His glory.

God Gave Us Dominion

The first command God gave to men and women was to be fruitful and multiply. The whole concept of marriage and family life is God's idea. It was He, who wanted us to fill the earth.

The KJV renders verse 28 as "replenish the earth". Some have used this to imply that the earth was being re-created, rather than created for the first time. This is the well-known Gap Theory, discussed earlier. In fact, to use this verse in this way is incorrect. There is nothing wrong with the KJV translation – it's just the English language that has changed. In the 17th century, when the KJV was translated, the word replenish did not mean to refill; it simply meant to fill.

God told us to subdue the world. He also told us to have dominion over it. This subjugation involves knowing about the world. This verse has often been called the *Cultural Mandate*. It is not stretching a point too far to say that this verse gives us license to practice science, art and technology. We need to study the world to subdue it. We need to harness its energy sources, to do useful work. And we need to exercise our own creativity. Our dominion over the world gives us the right to use the world, but also a responsibility. We do not have a *Gaia*-type link with the world. We are not to worship it. Industrialisation is not necessarily wrong, and is frequently the right exercise of our cultural mandate. But coupled with this is a responsibility for creation. As Christians – indeed, as a human race – we are to protect our environment. This is not because we see industrialisation as inherently bad, but because we have the responsibility that comes with dominion. Basically God is saying "the world and all its animals are yours to use. Don't mess them up."

This is what the Westminster Shorter Catechism has to say about the creation of man.

Q. 10. How did God create man?

A. God created man male and female, after his own image, in knowledge, righteousness, and holiness, with dominion over the creatures. [5]

Now, at the end of Day 6, God looks at all that He has made, including man, and He saw that "indeed it was **very** good". (v31 – emphasis mine). There is a slight difference. Before, as God looked over His world He saw it as good. Now He sees it as very good. The reason for the increase in strength of His declaration is that now the world is complete. He has reached the pinnacle of His creation. Everything in the six days of creation was leading up to this point – to put man in the world.

It is said that Copernicus removed Earth from the centre of the universe, and that Darwin removed him from the centre of history. I shouldn't equate Copernicus and Darwin, as one observed actual scientific phenomenon, whereas we believe the other was just plain wrong. But the Bible puts Earth back at the centre of the universe, metaphorically, if not actually, and it puts man at the centre of history. This world is here for a purpose. We are here for a purpose. Once again, the Shorter Catechism reminds us of that purpose.

Q. 1. What is the chief end of man?

A. Man's chief end is to glorify God, and to enjoy him forever.[6]

---

[5] Westminster Shorter Catechism, question 10.
[6] *Ibid.*

9.   Day Seven – God Rests

Read Genesis 2:1 – 3

Genesis tells us that God rested on the seventh day.

Those who believe that Genesis teaches long ages, rather than actual days, sometimes suggest that we are in the seventh day of rest now. God made the world over a long period of time, and now He is resting.

I find that view hard to accept. To begin with, as I have already stated, I accept the six days of creation as six literal days. Nowhere else in the Old Testament do conservative evangelical scholars worry about whether the word *yom* means day. As someone has once said, we do not spend time in our Bible studies worrying about whether Joshua marched the people around Jericho for six thousand years.

But there is another objection. In my view, God is not at rest today. He has intervened in history. I believe in the God of miracles. I believe that God actively stepped into my life, at the age of fifteen, when He saved me. And I believe that he intervened in history supremely, when God the Son, Jesus Christ, lived amongst us, died for our sins, and rose again from the dead. That is not a time of rest as I understand it.

Yet on this seventh day, God rested. In doing so, He set a pattern for us to follow. He looked at the world and universe He had made, and saw that it was very good. It was now complete and perfect. There was no death, or sin. Some people think that Satan had already become bad. How could he, when God declared the universe to be very good? Some say that God had taken millions of years to create the world. How could that be so, when millions of years implies the death of millions of creatures, in pain and suffering, yet God said the world was very good? Some people think that this account of creation was God recreating a world that He had previously destroyed. How could it be, if Adam and Eve walked over the fossils of dead creatures, and God said the world was very good?

If we accept that God made the world in six literal days, and rested on the seventh, we have the explanation for that anomalous period of time – the week.

All the other time periods are astronomical. They have naturalistic explanations. I still believe God made them, but scientists can look at them, and explain their observations.

The day is the period of rotation of the Earth on its axis. It can be measured, by the time period from when the Sun is highest in the sky, to the next time it is highest in the sky – noon to noon. The year is the time taken for the Earth to orbit the Sun. It can be measured by the seasons, or the procession and recession of the position of sunrise. The month is approximately the period of the Moon's orbit of the Earth. It can be measured by observing the phases of the Moon.

But there is no such naturalistic explanation of the week. And yet the week is important to us.

During the French Revolution, a calendar was introduced, in which a week was ten days. This proved unpopular – probably because a rest day once every ten days was not enough! Yet when the Soviets tried a six-day week with a rest day every six days - that did not catch on either. It seems that there is something about the way we are made that requires a seven day week, with a rest day every seven days. This should be no surprise to us, because it was God's idea. We move away from the concept of a seven day rhythm at our peril.

Yet today the concept of a rest day every seven days is losing popularity. Sunday has now become a shopping day and a work day. In the UK, changes in the Sunday trading laws, just over a decade ago, have caused problems for many families. In theory, no one can be forced to work on Sunday, but you try getting that job if you inform your prospective employees that you are unable to work on Sunday. The Lord's Day Observance Society have this to say:

Britain today is a sick nation and the trouble is largely psychological. Never have we had life so good, is the testimony of many. This country has still one of the highest standards of living in the world. Yet so many people have something wrong with them. They can't sleep. They can't rest. They take tranquillisers. They swallow pills by the bottle full. Cases that stem from mental and emotional instability fill vast numbers of our hospital beds. What on earth is the matter with us? We are told it is the pace of modern life. So it is. But God has directed that the pace should slacken to a stand-still once a week. But we think we know better. On we go regardless, restless and continually dissatisfied until the almost inevitable crash. The misuse of our Sunday lies very near the heart of the cause of all our problems.[1]

Read that quote again carefully, and few could doubt the truth of its case. As in so many areas, we are moving far away from God's word, and the laws that He has created for our own good. If a day's rest in seven was good enough for God, it is certainly good enough for us.

---

[1] Day One Magazine, September-December 2003, p23

10. The Garden of Eden

Read Genesis 2: 4 – 25

10.1.   Genesis, the History Book

4 This is the history of the heavens and the earth when they were created, in the day that the LORD God made the earth and the heavens,

Morris makes a convincing case that the first half of this verse, "is the history of the heavens and the earth when they were created" is actually the conclusion of the previous section, rather than the start of a new section.[1] Morris, in common with other commentators, surmises that the Book of Genesis was compiled by Moses from existing manuscripts. These manuscripts were written by characters at the time, and preserved or handed on, so that Moses had a true record, from which to compile the Book of Genesis.

The word translated as *history* above is the word *Toledoth*. This actually implies origins, or records of origins. In Genesis 5:1 and elsewhere, the same word is translated as "book of the genealogy". Each of these similar statements could be a signing off by the person concerned. This would perhaps appear to suggest nine possible subsections, according to Morris, compiled by Adam, Noah, Noah's sons, Shem, Terah, Isaac, Jacob and the sons of Jacob. The first section could only have been given by direct revelation of God.

None of the above is to deny that Moses is the author of Genesis. On the contrary, this writer is convinced that Moses wrote the first five books of the Bible, including Genesis. It is merely a suggestion of how Moses could have been made aware of events well before his lifetime.

Many other experts suggest that Genesis must have been given to Moses in one piece, by direct revelation from God. This suggestion also fits with the observations we make, and is an equally valid position to

---

[1] Morris, H., *The Genesis Record*, Evangelical Press: 1976, pp26ff

take.

The purpose for my making the above points is not to engage in a controversy about the origin of the inspiration of Genesis, but to emphasize very strongly that Genesis is to be treated as a true, historical account, and not as an allegorical or poetic work.

10.2. Genesis 2 in the scheme of Genesis 1

In the second half of Genesis 2:4, we have the Hebrew word *yom* or day being used to indicate a period of time. The context shows that it is a period of time rather than a 24 hour day. This does not undermine what we have said about the days of creation. On the contrary – it underlines the fact that day means day unless the context shows different. It also illustrates how easy it is to arrange the context to show a period of time rather than a 24 hour day. Thus there is no confusion. The days of Genesis 1 remain as literal days, because their context makes them 24 hour days.

> 5 before any plant of the field was in the earth and before any herb of the field had grown. For the LORD God had not caused it to rain on the earth, and there was no man to till the ground;

There are some scholars who tell us that Genesis 1 and Genesis 2 form two different accounts of creation. This is not the case. Genesis 2 is best understood as being an expansion of the account of Day 6.

This becomes more understandable, when we accept that they are in separate book-portions of the library that is Genesis. Genesis 1, we surmise was written directly by God and passed on to Moses. Genesis 2 was written by Adam. Neither contradicts the other, if we understand that Adam's concern is to amplify the nature of the creation of him and Eve.

God had made the plants according to their kind on day 3. Now on Day 6, God was filling the Earth. Apparently, the right purpose of the earth is to be subdued by mankind.

> 6 but a mist went up from the earth and watered the whole face of the ground.

The hydrological cycle must have been considerably different to what it is today. We are told that there was no rain. Indeed, we can expect that there would be no rain before the Flood. After the Flood, God sets His rainbow in the clouds. This illustrates that there was no rainbow before the Flood.

That there was no rain before the Flood makes perfect sense. Rain is caused by droplets of water condensing. These droplets need particles of dust, around which to coalesce. This dust would not have been available in God's perfect world, but would have been in abundance after the Flood, with the geological upheavals set off by the weight of water.

We also know that most of the Earth's surface was land before the Flood. That is why God separated the waters into one place and called them sea. We can envisage that the pre-diluvian geology would be entirely different. The Flood seems to have been caused mostly by the Fountains of the deep. Thus there must have been underground waterways, carrying water back and forth. This effect, combined with the mist over the land, would comprise the pre-diluvian hydrological cycle.

A great deal of work has gone into researching how this pre-diluvian hydrological cycle would work. It is worth checking the various peer-reviewed technical creationist journals, for more information on this fascinating subject.[2]

10.3.   God made Adam

7 And the LORD God formed man of the dust of the ground, and breathed into his nostrils the breath of life; and man became a living being.

We have discussed earlier the important concept of *nephesh*. Vertebrate animals, and possibly some invertebrate animals, have *nephesh*. Human beings have *nephesh*. This means that the life in animals is of a different type than that in plants. Plant death is not the

---

[2] For example, see Creation Research Society Quarterly (CRSQ) from the Creation Research Society (www.creationresearch.org) or CEN TJ (Creation Ex Nihilo Technical Journal) from Answers in Genesis (www.answersingenesis.org)

sort of death brought in by the Fall, because it is not soul death. We have also seen that mankind is created on an altogether higher level than the animals, because we are made in the image of God.

Now we learn that God's creation of Adam was even more special. The animals were created *ex nihilo*. Adam was not. He was created out of the dust of the earth. Through this, God reminds us that we are part of His creation, but have dominion over it. We are thoroughly connected to the material of the Earth, but the Earth was created for us to live on. God did not make the Earth *for* the animals, though they have a right to be there, and God has blessed them. It is only to us as human beings that God has given the purpose of dominion. "The Earth is the Lord's and everything in it", but He has granted us oversight.

Our *nephesh* life was breathed into Adam's nostrils directly by God. This makes our soul-life of a different order to that of the animals. We may see "personality" in a well-loved pet. It is, however, only temporary. It will end at the death of the animal. But our souls last for ever, because they are of the breath of God.

The breath of God is rightly seen as synonymous with the Spirit of God. The Holy Spirit plays such an important part in our lives. It is through the Holy Spirit that we have *nephesh* soul life in the first place. It is through the Holy Spirit that we are born again, when we give our lives to the Lord. And it is the Holy Spirit who empowers us and gifts us in our Christian lives.

10.4.   The Garden of Eden

8 The LORD God planted a garden eastward in Eden, and there He put the man whom He had formed.

9 And out of the ground the LORD God made every tree grow that is pleasant to the sight and good for food. The tree of life was also in the midst of the garden, and the tree of the knowledge of good and evil.

10 Now a river went out of Eden to water the garden, and from there it parted and became four riverheads.

11 The name of the first is Pishon; it is the one which skirts the whole land of Havilah, where there is gold.

12 And the gold of that land is good. Bdellium and the onyx stone are there.

13 The name of the second river is Gihon; it is the one which goes

around the whole land of Cush.
14 The name of the third river is Hiddekel; it is the one which goes toward the east of Assyria. The fourth river is the Euphrates.

God made a garden for Adam. We are given a little information about its geography, in that it is planted in the east. Beyond that, we cannot say much about its location.

The first thing we need to notice is that God planted it. He made it especially for people. It was to contain all the plant food necessary for us. And this food was not just nutritious. We also read that it was "pleasant to the sight and good for food". Why does food taste so good? Food doesn't need to taste good to do us good. But God has made us so that we can take pleasure in food. We can recognise gradations in food quality – some food is tastier than other food. Some people are better at cooking than other people. This is all part of the way God has made us.

The special planting of the garden shows that this was separate to and different from the creation of plants. Plants were created on Day 3. Here, in the middle of Day 6, God planted a garden, so that Adam's first experience of his Creator is as someone who loves him and cares for him.

The next thing we see is that God put two special trees in the garden. They are the tree of life and the tree of the knowledge of good and evil. This is the first mention of evil in the Bible. The tree of life is so powerful, that even a mortal man eating of it would live forever. It is interesting that the fruit of the tree of life will be available to us again one day, in the New Jerusalem that God puts in His New Heaven and New Earth.

It is very difficult to understand the tree of the knowledge of good and evil. It is not possible that the tree could itself actually be evil, or contain harmful substances. Otherwise, God could not have looked at the world and said it was very good. In C.S. Lewis's classic science fiction epic, "Perelandra", Lewis proposes a similar rule for the King and Queen of Venus. They were not to be allowed to stay overnight on the fixed island. It was suggested that this rule existed just for the sake of being obeyed. Lewis's idea is that a rule like not eating of the tree of knowledge of good and evil exists for its own sake. Otherwise God could not teach us obedience. It follows that the knowledge of evil, and its difference from good, are obtained by disobeying God, and eating of the tree.

We have no evidence whether or not there was anything dangerous in the fruit of the tree itself. The important point, as Lewis shows us, is that it was a test of Adam's obedience.

Next, we are given some information about the geography of Eden. We already know that it was to the East of where Adam was at his creation. Now we are told that there is a river in Eden. Presumably, this river rose in Eden, at a spring. Once out of Eden, the river splits into four rivers – the Pishon, Gihon, Hiddekel (otherwise known as the Tigris) and the Euphrates. The lands, through which these rivers flow, are described. We notice immediately a problem. Cush is the name given to the area we know today as Ethiopia. Yet we have here a river from the same source as the Tigris and the Euphrates. Although the Tigris and the Euphrates are close together, they do not spring from the same source.

The only reason these issues give us problems is because we forget what we are doing, and start to interpret everything from an evolutionary point of view. We believe, however, that the world was destroyed in the Flood. There is no reason to suppose that pre-diluvian geography is in any way related to post-diluvian geography.

So why do they have the same names as later biblical sites, or areas in the world today?

As a child growing up in Manchester, England's second city, I was intrigued that there were a couple of places called Manchester in the USA. These re-namings happen a lot. In the same way, I suggest that the post-diluvian Euphrates was simply named after the pre-diluvian Euphrates. This does not mean that it had any geographical relationship to the older river.

The whole of the Mesopotamian Crescent in modern Iraq is covered with sedimentary rock. The Tigris and Euphrates both flow over sedimentary rock. It is our contention that the majority of sedimentary rock was laid down in the Flood, so the current Tigris and Euphrates could not have been the same as those before the Flood.

10.5. Time for work

15 Then the LORD God took the man and put him in the garden of Eden to tend and keep it.

In the Garden, before sin had entered the world, man was supposed to work. Flanders and Swann used to sing "Heat is Work and Work's a curse!"[3] Today we are used to thinking that work is a problem that we need to get through. Yet in the sinless Garden, man was set to work. I heard a sermon on the subject of the Ten Commandments. When the preacher reached the commandment on not working on the Sabbath, he drew breath, then said "You are all expecting me to point out that God said we should rest one day in seven – and that is true. But notice that God says 'Six days you shall work!' – a commandment largely ignored in today's leisure based economy." It is true that after the Fall, as we shall discover, work became toil. Nevertheless, we worship God with our work, and the ability to do a good job, and to put every effort into it comes from God.

10.6.   The Wages of Sin...

16 And the LORD God commanded the man, saying, "Of every tree of the garden you may freely eat;
17 but of the tree of the knowledge of good and evil you shall not eat, for in the day that you eat of it you shall surely die."

We have already discussed a possible reason for God's law. At this juncture, it is important simply to note two facts

- God gave a law that man had to keep
- God declared a sanction for law-breaking

Man is made in the image of God, but man is not God. It follows that man is to obey God, because the creature must obey the creator. In a perfect world, how is man to obey God? In order for man to obey God, God must give a law for man to obey. Logic alone demands that we accept this. If we have no law, we have no yardstick, against which to measure our obedience.

---

[3] Flanders, Michael and Swann, Donald – "The Second Law of Thermodynamics Song" from "At the Drop of Another Hat", 1962

Paul said "The law was our tutor to bring us to Christ". (Galatians 3:24). In our present sinful state, the law exists to show us that it is not possible for us fully to obey God in our own strength. It points out our sinfulness. The word that the NKJV translates as *tutor* is in fact *pedagogue*. In Greek culture, a pedagogue was a very special type of educator. As the student walked around in the grounds of the school, reading his books, the pedagogue walked behind (hence *peda* – feet) carrying a big stick. Every time the student lost concentration, the pedagogue would hit him with a stick. The law has the same effect on us. The law itself cannot save us, argues Paul. It exists simply as a measure of our obedience, and a stick, with which to beat us when we fail. As we know, true justification is found by faith in Jesus Christ.

, Some theologians have pondered about whether God should have made Adam incapable of sinning. Why did God allow sin into the world? I don't know the answer to this. But I do know that a world, in which man was incapable of obeying God *by an act of his own will* would not have been "very good". God did not design Adam to be a robot, but to be in the image of God. It follows that the giving of this one law for Adam to obey meant that Adam had the ability to choose whether or not to obey. To suppose less would be to make Adam less than human, and to make the created world less than very good.

So we have a logical progression of thought. God made Adam in His image. Adam's job was to worship God, including working. This worship includes obeying God. In order to obey God, Adam needed to be given a law to keep. If Adam was given a law to keep, then he must have been capable of obedience or disobedience. Finally, if Adam was able to disobey God, he needed to be informed of the consequences of his disobedience. Nothing was kept secret from Adam in this. God said "in the day that you eat of it you shall surely die." As Paul said in Romans 6:23 "For the wages of sin is death..." The appropriate punishment for sin is declared to be death.

For the Christian who believes in evolution, or in progressive creation, they have a problem. I often wondered about this verse in my youth. I wondered about the inconsistency. Because, when Adam did actually sin, he did not die.

For those of us who take Genesis seriously, there is no inconsistency. If Adam had not sinned, he would not have died. Genesis 2:17 uses a continuous type of tense. Literally, the phrase should read, "Dying, you will die". Adam began to die physically at the moment he sinned. Spiritually, he died immediately, because he was cut off from the presence of God. From that point on, his physical death was inevitable. The fact that he lived another 930 years is irrelevant. If he had not sinned, he would still have been alive today, and would have gone on living forever. In dying, he died.

10.7.   Man Gave Names to All the Animals

18 And the LORD God said, "It is not good that man should be alone; I will make him a helper comparable to him."
19 Out of the ground the LORD God formed every beast of the field and every bird of the air, and brought them to Adam to see what he would call them. And whatever Adam called each living creature, that was its name.
20 So Adam gave names to all cattle, to the birds of the air, and to every beast of the field. But for Adam there was not found a helper comparable to him.

God's world is still not yet complete. God didn't say the creation was very good until after he had created man as *male and female*. It follows that our account is still not at the end of Day 6. God hasn't yet made woman. That is why God could look at this aspect of His creation and say "it is not good". Notice that He didn't say it was bad. But He certainly cannot at this point say it is good, and certainly not very good.

I have often wondered why God now gave Adam the task of naming the animals. Notice that there is no implication that Adam completed his naming of the animals all on Day 6. The account simply tells us that Adam named them. It is perfectly possible that this task could have taken a lot longer than the length of this first day of Adam's existence. Notice also that, unlike the Bob Dylan song title I have used for this subsection, Adam did not give names to **all** the animals at this juncture – just the cattle, beasts of the field and birds. Creeping things, and marine creatures would have to wait for their names.

There is also no contradiction between verse 19 and Genesis Chapter 1. The context is not implying that the animals were made at this point. They had been made earlier. It was at this point that God started to bring the animals to Adam.

The purpose of this strange interlude suggests two things.

In naming the animals, Adam was understanding them. This demonstrates his remarkable intelligence. Evolutionists believe that our intelligence is on the increase. While our technology may indeed be increasing, and the sum total of our knowledge may be increasing, because of the passage of years, there is no evidence to suggest that we are more intelligent today, than our ancestors. Indeed, as we look at our more recent past, we see that 19th Century scientists were arguably intellectually far superior to today's scientists, but their available technology was more primitive. Adam was naming the animals before six thousand years of the curse had affected human brains. It is my contention that his intellectual capacity was far beyond ours.

The second suggestion is this; God is emphasising to Adam that he is not the same as the animals. Eve was not just a semi-evolved simian, for Adam to think "Oh, that's close enough, I'll marry it"! Adam found no companion among the animals. God never intended that he would. God always intended to make Eve. But this passage proves that we did not evolve from lower animals. Man was separately created, and given dominion. He is unique in creation.

10.8.   Male and Female He Created Them

21 And the LORD God caused a deep sleep to fall on Adam, and he slept; and He took one of his ribs, and closed up the flesh in its place.
22 Then the rib which the LORD God had taken from man He made into a woman, and He brought her to the man.
23 And Adam said: "This is now bone of my bones And flesh of my flesh; She shall be called Woman, Because she was taken out of Man."
24 Therefore a man shall leave his father and mother and be joined to his wife, and they shall become one flesh.
25 And they were both naked, the man and his wife, and were not ashamed.

The deep sleep that came on Adam is mentioned elsewhere in the Bible. One such place is the giving of the covenant to Abraham, in Genesis 15. Abram, as he then was, divides his sacrificial animals, but then he is in a deep sleep, and can take no part in the covenant with God.

This is because it is a one-sided covenant. In the same way, Eve was to be at the heart of a covenantal relationship with Adam and with God, both in the institution of marriage, and in her relationship to God as co-heir, equal with Adam.

It is entirely logical that God should make Eve from Adam, rather than making her in the same way He made Adam. If Eve had been separately created, then she would have been a representative of all women. Some liberal theologians talk about a race of women and a race of men, with the story of Adam and Eve being an allegory of their meeting. If that were so, then Eve would separately represent women, and women today would need another representative – a female Messiah. However, Eve was made from Adam, so that she contained related genetic material. Adam originally contained all the genetic material of the human race. He therefore represented the **whole** human race – men and women. Therefore we need a Last Adam; a new representative, Jesus Christ. Jesus is the new Adam, representing all of us, both men and women.

If God had made Eve first, there would be the suggestion that Adam was *born* rather than separately created. Therefore men and women would not be equal in the sight of God. Despite how many commentators have twisted these issues, the account of Eve being created from Adam's side shows that she was equal in the sight of God, and yet Adam could remain her representative, just as Jesus is our representative today.

The present passage is fundamental to a Biblical understanding of marriage. Marriage is to be a partnership of one man and one woman. This partnership is supposed to be permanent. That is why it is said that a man leaves his father and mother. Leaving the parental home is a major step for any young person. Ultimately, this is to be for the purpose of setting up a new family home with husband or wife.

As an aside, it is noteworthy that Jesus quotes passages from both Genesis chapters one and two when defining His teaching on marriage. It follows that Jesus saw no separation between these two chapters, but rather viewed them as a consistent whole. That is to be our attitude in interpreting Genesis, and is one of the main reasons why we reject the theory that chapters 1 and 2 relate two different creation accounts.

11. A Brief History of Satan

Read Genesis 3:1a

Now the serpent was more cunning than any beast of the field, which the LORD God had made.

One of the most puzzling conundrums of the Bible is where Satan came from, and how evil was released into the world. As we study into chapter 3 of Genesis, we will discover how sin affected humankind and the universe as a whole. But it will be worthwhile pausing to see how evil came to be in the world at all. A number of statements regarding the person of Satan need to be made.

11.1. Satan, the Devil and the Serpent are the same

Revelation makes this point very clear. "He (that is an angel from heaven) laid hold of the dragon, that serpent of old, who is the Devil and Satan..." (Revelation 20:2). This originator of evil is one person. He has helpers, but there is one devil opposed to Jesus Christ.

11.2. Satan is a person

Dualism teaches that there is an impersonal force in the universe, divided into good and evil components. Although this idea has been around for millennia, it has gained popularity in recent decades, through the medium of the Star Wars films. Even though they are intended to be entertainment, they seem to resonate with prevailing views of Good and Evil as equal and opposite forces. I am constantly amazed at the number of those, who call themselves Christians, who do not believe in a personal devil. Make no mistake. The devil is not an impersonal force.

He is a person who desires you harm, especially if you profess the name of Jesus. He speaks, even if he has disguised himself, or possessed an animal like the serpent. Quite how the serpent spoke we do not know. The passage in Revelation quoted above shows that the serpent is in fact considered to be the devil, rather than the devil simply possessing an animal. I am not able to be dogmatic on this subject, except to point out that the devil speaks personally.

11.3. The Devil was evil from the Beginning

"You are of your father the devil, and the desires of your father you want to do. He was a murderer from the beginning, and does not stand in the truth, because there is no truth in him. When he speaks a lie, he speaks from his own resources, for he is a liar and the father of it." (John 8:44)

Notice that the passage describes the devil as being evil from the beginning, not from before the beginning. That is because:

11.4. Satan was created good

When God looked at the world He had made, with humans in it, He said it as **very good**. If he devil had already been evil, then the world would not have been very good. So whenever we believe the Fall of Satan happened, it could not have been before or during the six days of creation.It is more likely that Satan's Fall happened shortly before he started to tempt Eve.

It goes without saying, therefore, that Satan was created. In Ezekiel 28:12ff, we read, "Thus says the Lord God: 'You were the seal of perfection, full of wisdom and perfect in beauty. You were in den, the garden of God.'" This passage, about the King of Tyre, seems to be addressing an angelic being – most likely to be Satan himself. "You were the anointed cherub who covers; I established you".

A similar passage about an angelic being called Lucifer (or morning star) is described by Isaiah. "How you are fallen from heaven, O Lucifer, son of the morning!". The reason for this Fall – "For you have said in your heart 'I will ascend into heaven, I will exalt my throne above the stars of God."

11.5. Satan is dangerous and powerful

Be sober, be vigilant; because your adversary the devil walks about like a roaring lion, seeking whom he may devour. (1 Peter 5:8)

11.6. Satan has lost; Jesus has won

But thanks be to God, who gives us the victory through our Lord Jesus Christ. (1 Corinthians 15:57).

The whole point of the Gospel is that Jesus has the victory. In Revelation, we read that Satan is ultimately to be thrown into the Lake of Fire.

This is, then, the brief history of Satan. He is to be treated with a wary respect, as did the Archangel Michael, as described in the letter of Jude, but we must equally remember that he is a defeated enemy. Thanks be to God.

12. Temptation and Fall

Read Genesis 3:1 – 8

There is a sickening pattern to the manner, in which Satan tempted Eve, and it is a pattern we would do well to remember today, because Satan employs the same tricks and exploits the same weaknesses.

12.1. Temptation 1 – Doubting God's Word

The first thing Satan says to Eve is "Has God indeed said?" or, in other words, "Did God really say…?". His first attack is to sow the seeds of doubt. There should have been no doubt in Eve's mind. If God has said something to us, then we had better make sure we know what it is.

Today, Satan's first attack on us is to get us to doubt God's word. So many individual Christians and churches have fallen at this first hurdle. For many people, God's word is not taken at face value.

At one extreme we have those who believe the Bible has been proved to be in error. We need not concern ourselves with that argument at this juncture, not because it is not important, but because it is probably not the issue concerning readers of this book, and in any case, the issue has been dealt with more effectively elsewhere.

Then there are those who tell us that they believe the Bible *contains* the truth. In a spiritual sense, they inform us, we can accept the basic truth behind the Bible, without believing it all really happened.

Caught drifting down this same road are those who believe the Bible to be true, but cannot accept the book of Genesis as scientific or historical fact. Those who misinterpret the Bible in this way are, as we have discussed earlier, opening the floodgates for all sorts of unbiblical errors to creep in.

12.2. Temptation 2 – Misquoting God

"Has God indeed said, 'You shall not eat of every tree of the garden'?"

Satan's second line of attach is to misquote God's word. Satan knew very well that this was not what God had said. There is a subtle difference between saying "You shall not eat of every tree" and saying "Here is a tree, from which you shall not eat." Some might argue that the meaning is the same. That is the argument of Alice in Wonderland at the Mad Hatter's Tea Party. One is a specific, easily followed command. The other is an unspecific, possibly confusing injunction. It is part of Satan's lies that he tries to confuse us about the truth.

Eve should have been better versed in what God said. However, she ends up misquoting God herself. "We may eat the fruit of the trees of the garden; but of the fruit of the tree which is in the midst of the garden, God has said, 'You shall not eat it, *nor shall you touch it*, lest you die.'" God did not say the portion in italics. Eve has allowed her own interpretation of the word to creep in.

So many errors in understanding the Bible come about because people add to what it says, either accidentally or deliberately. To avoid accidental misunderstanding of the Bible, we need to understand what it says. To know and understand what it says, we need to read it. This last point is so basic, that it seems strange that so many Christians have missed it. Yet time and again, I meet Christians who do not read the Bible every day. It is so important to read a portion of God's word every day. That is the only way to know what it says. Sometimes, if I have tried to explain something from the Bible, other Christians will ask me "How do you know all that?" I reply that it is no trick, and there is no secret. I have just been reading the Bible for nearly thirty years. It doesn't take intelligence. If you can read, you can know the Bible. No, that's not right – you don't even have to be able to read. Today, we can get the Bible on tape, and listen. One of the most godly men I have ever met was an illiterate man, who remembered every sermon he had heard, and remembered what verses were being read, and he loved to talk endlessly with people about the God he loved! Yet today there are Christians who do not touch the Bible from one Sunday to the next, and often don't even take their Bibles to church with them. How would they have fited in the

Berean church, where the members "searched the Scriptures daily to find out whether these things were so" – the things that Paul and Silas were telling them (Acts 17:11). As for scripture memory – what has happened to that? No one memorises scripture anymore. It is such a blessing to me that when I was at university, some friends persuaded me to go through the Navigator's Topical Memory System. The verses that I memorised from that scheme have stayed with me ever since. You see, Satan tempts us when we haven't got an expert Christian stood next to us, to demolish his arguments for us. He attacks when we are alone, and unguarded. Don't leave your souls unguarded. Have the words of scripture to quote back at him, to send him away. "Resist the devil and he will flee from you." (James 4:7)

12.3. Temptation 3 – Contradicting God

Now that Satan has confused Eve, Caused her to doubt, and to mix up the words God had given, he is now able to launch his weapon of mass destruction. "You will not surely die." He is ready to contradict God directly. Some people are worried that soft drugs lead inevitably to hard drugs. Soft temptation, if it is entertained and not resisted, leads to hard temptation. Satan could not start by contradicting God, but now that he has got Eve confused and doubting, he is ready to contradict God to her.

I used to wonder about Satan's comments here. Wasn't he telling the truth? God had said about the tree of knowledge "in the day that you eat of it you shall surely die." But they didn't die, did they? In fact, the Hebrew uses a form that could be more correctly translated as "In dying, you shall die." The whole process of dying, which would lead inevitably to death, would begin, the moment they broke His command. This is indeed what happened, and Satan's comments can be seen to be lies. Adam and Eve would not have died if they had not sinned. Because they sinned, the process of death began, for Adam and the whole world – but more of that later.

So many errors come about because Christians have allowed worldly philosophies to contradict what God says. It is easier for a quiet life to go along with what the world says, yet the Apostle John exhorts us: "Do not love the world or the things in the world. If anyone loves the world, the love of the Father is not in him. For all that is in the world——the lust of the flesh, the lust of the eyes, and the pride of life - is not of the Father but is of the world." (1 John 2:15,16).

It is these lusts that are at the centre of Satan's subtle temptations.

12.4. Temptation 4 – Being Jealous of God

"God knows that in the day you eat of it your eyes will be opened, and you will be like God, knowing good and evil."

Satan appeals to our pride. He tells us that we can be like God. He flatters us, knowing that this was never what God had in mind for the best for our well-being.

This is indeed the sin caused Satan's Fall in the first place.

For you have said in your heart: 'I will ascend into heaven, I will exalt my throne above the stars of God; I will also sit on the mount of the congregation On the farthest sides of the north; I will ascend above the heights of the clouds, I will be like the Most High.' (Isaiah 14:13,14)

Satan has failed to become like God, but it is jealousy of God that directs his every move. It is that jealousy, with which he tempts us.

12.5. The Guilt and Shame

Read Genesis 3:8 - 13

The saddest verse in the opening three chapters of Genesis is verse 8.

And they heard the sound of the LORD God walking in the garden in the cool of the day, and Adam and his wife hid themselves from the presence of the LORD God among the trees of the garden.

The two human beings, who were directly created by God, enjoyed fellowship with God, as He walked around in the Garden. Suddenly this fellowship is broken. Adam and Eve can no longer enter the presence of God, so they hide from Him.

If verse 8 is the saddest verse, verse 10 is one of the most pathetic. "So he (Adam) said, 'I heard Your voice in the garden, and I was afraid because I was naked; and I hid myself.'" This was the first feeble excuse ever made by a human being to God, but it was not the last. We know that God knows everything about us. When He asks us a question, like He does of Adam in verse 9 – "Where are you?" – the question is for our benefit, not His. He knows the answer, but He was drawing Adam out, so that Adam would see for himself the consequences of his actions. We will never know what would have happened if Adam had jumped out of hiding, and fallen on his knees before God in repentance. Instead, he looks for excuses. "How like a man!" I have heard others remark. Yes – how like a man – but I am using the term in its non-sexist connotation of mankind. How like a human being! How like you and me not to face up to our responsibility, but to hide behind the feeblest of excuses.

Nakedness was not a sin at the beginning. Genesis 2:25 tells us "And they were both naked, the man and his wife, and were not ashamed." Nakedness had never previously been a hindrance to fellowship with God. It was their shame and guilt, due to their sin, that caused their nakedness to be a problem.

Adam and Eve attempted to sort out this problem themselves. They made themselves coverings out of fig-leaves. This solution was not sufficient, and we will learn more later about God's better remedy. For now, we should note that Adam and Eve were attempting to cover up their guilt by their fashioning of fig-leaf garments. We should also note that they still felt the need to hide. Their attempts to atone for their own guilt was a failure – it did not stop them feeling guilty and ashamed in the presence of God.

Again, God gives Adam the opportunity to repent. Again, we don't know what would have happened if he had done so. "Have you eaten from the tree of which I commanded you that you should not eat?" So we, as readers, are willing Adam to say, "Yes, Lord, I ate from the tree. I have sinned and I repent." God's question also serves to remind Adam of the one and only command that God had given him. Sin is a transgression of God's law. Sin is not committed in a vacuum, or in secret. Now was Adam's opportunity to admit the nature of his sin. But instead we have an even more pathetic excuse – Adam attempts to shift the blame.

"The woman whom You gave to be with me, she gave me of the tree, and I ate."

It is Eve's fault, according to Adam, because she gave him the fruit. Even worse, it is partly God's fault, because You gave Eve to be with me, God! It is anyone's fault but Adam's. There are only two people in the whole world, but Adam still wants to blame someone else.

Eve was not responsible for Adam's sin, as we have noted several times already. She was not Adam's representative. When Eve sinned, it was her own sin. Adam, however, was our representative. Unlike Eve, he was not deceived by Satan. In other words, he knew exactly what he was doing. His was the greater sin, and his sin was imputed to you and me.

Adam's foolish comments are not to go unregarded by God, but for the moment, he moves on to question Eve. She also has the opportunity to repent. She does not. She also engages in the art of blame-shifting. She blames the serpent, who of course, is guilty, but he is guilty of his own sin, not Eve's. Again, Eve's sin is not to go unnoticed, but for the moment God addresses the sin of the serpent.

13. The Curse

Read Genesis 3: 14 – 24

There now follow three curses. God declares a curse on the serpent, the man and the woman. There is a slight difference between each type of curse, commensurate with the nature of the sin and sinner concerned. We start with the curse on the serpent.

13.1. The Curse on the Serpent

The curse has two aspects. There is a curse on the serpent in its animal form, and there is a curse which is specifically directed at Satan. The two aspects of the curse are interrelated. As discussed earlier, we are not sure how Satan's appearance as a serpent was achieved. We can, however, assume that prior to the Fall, serpents had legs. The fact that snakes today do not have legs, but crawl on their bellies, is a visible reminder to us of what happened in the Garden. This does not make snakes any more evil than other animals, as many Christians who love keeping snakes as pets would testify! Something in nature can be a sign or a witness to us, without this being detrimental to the nature of the item itself. For instance, the stars in the sky point towards God's glory, say the psalms. This is not affected by our knowing that they are balls of hot gas, radiating light and heat through space. In the same way, snakes can be to us a reminder of the absolute truth of Genesis, without the snakes themselves being evil creatures.

However, the main thrust of God's curse on the serpent is at the person of Satan. One thing we should notice is that God's curse on the serpent allows no appeal, and no possibility of redemption for the serpent. As we shall see, redemption is offered to Adam and Eve, but not to Satan. The Bible is not like Eastern mystical religions, believing in a dualism – equal forces of Good and Evil. There is no equality between Satan and God. Satan is a created being. As a created angel, Satan had no representative, and he represents no one but himself. There is therefore no salvation for Satan and his angels, because there can be no Messiah to represent the entire evil portion of the angels. There is no angelic race. All angels are separately created.

> And I will put enmity between you and the woman, and between your seed and her Seed; He shall bruise your head, and you shall bruise His heel.

This part of the curse is terrible for Satan, but precious for us. God promises enmity between the serpent and the woman. This is shown in the irrational fear that many people have for snakes. But there is a greater spiritual significance. The passage goes on to talk about the Seed of the woman. In Revelation 12, we read about the woman giving birth to a male child. Henry Morris shows that this passage in Revelation is clearly linked to the passage in Genesis under discussion.[1] Morris shows that the woman in question is Israel. The man-child is Jesus. In the Revelation passage, the dragon tries to devour the child, without success. The nature of the dragon is revealed in Rev 12:9 "So the great dragon was cast out, that serpent of old, called the Devil and Satan, who deceives the whole world; he was cast to the earth, and his angels were cast out with him".

In the curse of Genesis 3, God shows that the woman and the serpent will be at enmity. This is because Satan wants to devour the man-child – the Messiah. God is promising the Messiah, right at the beginning of time, immediately after the first sin. Then we learn more about the nature of the Messiah. He is to be the seed of the woman. Anyone with a slight knowledge of biology knows that the seed is from the man, not the woman. God is promising that at some point in history there will be a seed of a woman; that the promised Messiah will be born of a woman, and thus fully human, **but with no human father!** This is a clear promise of the Virgin Birth. Mary was a Virgin, but became with child by the Holy Spirit and gave birth to Jesus. He is the fulfilment of the promise, which God is making, in the hearing of Adam and Eve, at the beginning of things. Doesn't it show the mercy of God that He gave us the Gospel immediately after the first sin. There has always been a way of salvation.

God goes on to show that the Messiah will be damaged by Satan – His heel will be bruised, but that Satan will be completely defeated by

---

[1] Morris, H.M., (1983), The Revelation Record, Tyndale: pp213ff

the Messiah – He will crush your head.

13.2. The Curse on the Woman

"I will greatly multiply your sorrow and your conception; In pain you shall bring forth children; Your desire shall be for your husband, And he shall rule over you."

This curse is of a more general nature, and does not cause an irredeemable state. It is a fact that childbirth can be a difficult and painful process. There is also a change in the natural order of things. The ideal state is for man and woman to be co-heirs, co-equals. There is nothing in this passage that prevents us striving for that. Remember, this is a curse, not a command. Over the ages, Christians have misinterpreted this verse as declaring the *rightness* of women's inferiority to men. In fact, the opposite is being stated. God is saying that there will be natural tendency for men to rule over women, but that in fact this is not how matters were intended to be. It takes positive effort to overcome this state of affairs, as the struggle of women throughout the 20th Century for equal rights has shown. The struggle for equal rights for women and men is a good thing. This curse merely explains that something went very wrong to cause the world to be unequal.

13.3. The Curse on the Man

We have seen before that Adam's sin is of infinitely greater import than Eve's sin. Adam sinned as our representative, so the curse on him is a curse on all humankind.

In fact, the curse on Adam affects the entire universe. It is at this point that death and decay enter the world. The ground itself is now cursed. The full force of the Second Law of Thermodynamics comes into play.

The Second Law of thermodynamics shows that in every energy change, some energy is always wasted, usually in the form of low temperature heat. Some aspects of the Second Law must already have been in place – after all, there must have been friction. But a lot of our understanding of the Second Law is as a mechanism causing the Universe to run down, like a wound-up clock. Death and decay are part of this process. Romans 8:20-22 shows how this curse has affected the whole universe.

> For the creation was subjected to futility, not willingly, but because of Him who subjected it in hope; because the creation itself also will be delivered from the bondage of corruption into the glorious liberty of the children of God. For we know that the whole creation groans and labours with birth pangs together until now.

The whole Earth is now cursed. Instead of work, we have toil. Work becomes something difficult. Even working the ground becomes difficult, because now the earth brings forth thorns and thistles. There were no thorns and thistles before the Fall. There are many fossils of thorns and thistles. This shows that none of the fossil record could have been produced before the Fall.

Food is obtained through toil and sweat. And death is inevitable – "For dust you are, And to dust you shall return." For all man's ingenuity, apart from God, there is no meaning to a man's life anymore, because ultimately we die, and return to the chemicals, from which we are composed. The greatest artist, the greatest musician, the greatest scientist, the greatest philosopher – all return to dust when they die. This is why Qohellet, the teacher, describes life as meaningless, or vanity.

> For what happens to the sons of men also happens to animals; one thing befalls them: as one dies, so dies the other. Surely, they all have one breath; man has no advantage over animals, for all is vanity. All go to one place: all are from the dust, and all return to dust. Who knows the spirit of the sons of men, which goes upward, and the spirit of the animal, which goes down to the earth? So I perceived that nothing is better than that a man should rejoice in his own works, for that is his heritage. For who can bring him to see what will happen after him? (Ecclesiastes 3:19-22)

After Adam had named his wife Eve, we read a remarkable verse, easily overlooked. "Also for Adam and his wife the LORD God made tunics of skin, and clothed them." Adam and Eve had tried to cover their nakedness themselves, by stitching together fig-leaves. We cannot cover our own guilt and shame, however, so they could not enter into God's presence, but had to hide. Now we read that God made them tunics of skin. Up to this point, no animal had died. People ate only plants. But now God kills animals to make tunics. We don't know what sort of animals God killed, but it must have been the sort of animals that give good clothing skin. Maybe it is reading too much into the passage to suggest that the animals could have been lambs. What is certain, however, is that blood was spilt in order to hide Adam and Eve's nakedness, guilt and shame. To be able to stand in the presence of God, required the shedding of blood. "And according to the law almost all things are purified with blood, and without shedding of blood there is no remission." (Hebrews 9:22) Once again, we have a glimpse of the gospel. We shall get a similar glimpse in Genesis chapter 4. God makes the way back to himself. God himself provides the sacrifice, as He did for Abraham and Isaac. One day, God the Father was to sacrifice His only Son, the perfect Lamb of God, on the cross, so that we can stand guiltless and without shame before the throne of God.

14. Sin, Murder and Worship

Read Genesis 3:23 – 4:26

14.1. Banished from Eden

A new episode in the life of Adam and Eve begins in chapter 3:23. Following their sin, they can no longer remain in the Garden of Eden. God, therefore, banishes them. They leave with a purpose. God's purpose for Adam is that he should work, tilling the ground.

Just because a new phase had opened in Adam's life did not mean that he was not responsible for obeying God. God is still to be in charge of Adam's life and work. We still have a responsibility to serve God through every aspect of our life and work.

God then placed Cherubim to guard the way to the tree of life. Adam had lost the right to eat of the tree of life – a right that will be restored to us when God recreates a New Heaven and New Earth.

Until the Flood came to destroy the Earth as it was, the Garden of Eden must have still been present. It was necessary for God to prevent physically humans from re-entering it. Why couldn't God have simply removed it? God could have destroyed it if He had wanted. I assume that the continued existence of the Garden, the Tree and the Cherubim served as a visible reminder to pre-diluvian people of what they had lost by their sin.

14.2. Children of Adam and Eve

The act of sexual intercourse for a married couple is described here as *knowing*. There is no closer way for a husband and wife to know each other. This is why the Bible makes clear that this act is only for within a married relationship. The phrase "Adam knew Eve" is not a quaint archaism, but a statement of correct morality. Others are more qualified than I to expound this aspect of the message, so I will add no more, save simply to confirm that Genesis is foundation to the Bible's moral teaching, as well as its doctrinal teaching.

Eve's declaration on giving birth to firstborn, Cain, is significant. She was no doubt remembering the words of God, promising that her seed would crush Satan. That is why the child was named Cain, which means "a possession". Eve declares "I have acquired a man from the LORD." What a disappointment that Cain was not to turn out to be the promised Saviour. Approximately four millennia were to pass before the true Saviour was to arrive.

Later, Adam and Eve have a second son, Abel. Abel means a breath or vapour. No doubt his parents were thinking of the breath of life from God, yet the name is prophetic of his brief time on Earth and how it was to cruelly cut short, as he became the first murder victim.

Before we examine the subject of Cain and Abel in more detail, let us make a further comment on the children of Adam and Eve. In Genesis 4, the narrative jumps straight to Cain and Abel being of age, able to work at their respective activities. We can assume that Adam and Eve did not wait to have more children. Indeed, we get the impression that Eve conceived Cain at the first attempt, so to speak. Although the world had been polluted by Adam's sin, the deterioration of the world was still at an early stage. Few genetic problems had yet arisen. Later in Genesis, we find that Sarah is barren. Barrenness was not yet an issue. Consider also the length of time that Adam and Eve were to live, and we see that it is realistic to suppose that they had very many children. Sons and daughters are mentioned in Gen 5:4. The NIV is correct in translating this as "other sons and daughters", so the three sons mentioned by name, Cain, Abel and Seth, were not the only sons of Adam and Eve, and there must have been many unnamed daughters. We will examine the influence of this fact on the population, and the effect and veracity of the ages given in Genesis, when we examine chapter 5. It will, however, be necessary for the understanding of chapter 4 to note that there would have been a large number of other children of both sexes.

14.3. Cain and Abel make offerings

It took me many, many years to understand the import of Genesis 4:3-7. How could God be so unfair to accept Abel's offering and not Cain's? Wasn't God partly to blame for this dreadful murder?

Of course, the answer must be different. An infinitely good God has not made a mistake in His acceptance, and nor is He showing capriciousness. Indeed, the clue to why one offering is acceptable and the other not has already been given.

There is a slight clue in the description of the brothers in verse 2. "Now Abel was a keeper of sheep, but Cain was a tiller of the ground." Why is the word "but" used? (Incidentally, the word used in the NIV is "and", which seems to be in error.) There was nothing wrong in tilling the ground. This was the work that Adam had been assigned, even before the Fall. If the Bible is suggesting there was something wrong with Cain tilling the ground, then it is not the action of tilling which is wrong, but rather the way that Cain tilled the ground.

Eventually, Cain brings an offering to the Lord from his crops. This is the work that he has done for himself. It is as if he is saying that God should be grateful for a portion of the work that Cain himself had done. This offering was not respected by God.

Abel's offering was the firstborn of his flock. In order to make this offering, he had to kill the lamb. It is possible that Abel less in value than Cain. The difference is that Abel was not trying to save himself, as Cain was. The clue we have already had is in the clothing of Adam and Eve. Adam and Eve tried to cover their own guilt and shame with fig leaves. God, however, covered their nakedness by shedding blood. Abel did likewise – the firstborn lamb was sacrificed in place of Abel's sin. The NIV says that God looked with favour on Abel's sacrifice. In Hebrews 11, we read that this was a more excellent sacrifice – note that the sacrifice is not merely *better* – it is *more excellent*. It is because forgiveness is only attained by the shedding of blood that was perfectly demonstrated by the shedding of the blood of God's only begotten Son. In a word, the acceptability of Abel's offering and non-acceptability of Cain's is down to the blood. We cannot save ourselves, as Cain tried to do. Our work for God is very good and proper, but it never saves us. We are saved only by the blood of sacrifice. Today that is the perfect sacrifice of Jesus. It is only through the perfect sacrifice of Jesus that we are accepted. This was the hard lesson that Cain was being taught. That is why God addresses Cain directly on the subject. Cain is angry that his sacrifice is not acceptable, but God is pointing him towards the attitude of his heart.

> If you do well, will you not be accepted? And if you do not do well, sin lies at the door. And its desire is for you, but you should rule over it.

God is an ever loving, ever forgiving God. He has not condemned Cain. He is offering Cain the way of salvation. Unfortunately, it is a way that Cain refuses to take. Instead, he decides to blame his brother for the incident. In no way could Abel be said to responsible for Cain's offering being rejected. We are all responsible for our own souls before God. Abel could not have made Cain acceptable to God. That is between God and Cain. Nevertheless, Cain cannot bring himself to blame himself. In that, he behaves like so many people today. It is out of his selfishness, pride and rebellion that he plans to commit the first murder. Whether the murder was pre-meditated or not, we do not know, but I suspect that it was. The NIV has it that Cain suggested to Abel that they go out to the field.

Having committed the world's first murder, Cain immediately tries to lie to God. Does he really think that God hasn't seen what he has done? It is possible that Cain's view of God is not what it should be. We have seen that Cain does not have the faith to offer sacrifice, trying to make himself right with God by his own strength. It is possible that Cain at least half believes that he can get away with this murder.

But the closeness of God to Cain in this whole story shows that there is no getting away from him. As Paul tells the pagan Athenians in Acts 17:27, "He is not far from each one of us." Just because we behave as if God is far off does not mean that He is. In fact, He is right there in the midst of things, as we commit sins. He sees our shame, but offers us His forgiveness.

There comes a point when our rejection of God can become permanent, however. Cain has now reached that point. He has been offered acceptance, but has refused the wonderful love of God. For the rest of his days on earth he is now to be cursed, and then to spend his eternity in hell. Cain is now cursed by a wanderlust – he will never be at home wherever he goes.

Cain is, too late, overwhelmed by his punishment. "It is greater than I can bear". Indeed it is not. God does not test us beyond what we can endure. Suddenly, Cain becomes concerned that he, himself, might be killed. By whom might he be killed? There must by now have been other sons and daughters of Adam, and possibly grandsons and granddaughters etc. But God gives Cain a mark to protect him. What could that mark have been? We have no evidence. Whatever it was, it prevented others from killing Cain.

Notice that Cain's journey did not just take him to the land of Nod. Clearly there was an earthly direction to his journey – Eastwards away from Eden. More significantly, however, Cain "went out from the presence of the Lord". The offer of salvation is now far from him. Readers of this book note this; it is possible to take yourself away from the presence of the Lord. He will not force you to be saved. But if you remove yourself from His presence, you may find you are never able to come back.

14.4. Cain's Wife

Much of the remainder of chapter 4 talks about Cain's descendents. Before this, however, we have a conundrum.

Who was Cain's wife?

Ken Ham says that he sometimes finds himself talking about Cain's wife more than about his own wife![36] The problem that is implicit in the question is this: Cain and Abel, Adam and Eve are the only humans mentioned so far. Aha, say the sceptics. There must have been other hominid creatures around. In other words, Adam and Eve were not unique, and maybe humans evolved after all.

Answers in Genesis have published an excellent and inexpensive little booklet dealing with this issue in detail.[37] The key to the solution of this

---

[36] Ham, Ken, **Reconnecting the Bible to the Real World**, (audio tape recording), Answers in Genesis Ministries (www.answersingenesis.org)

[37] **Answers to the Four Big Questions**, Answers in Genesis Minstries. The booklet also contains answers to the questions "But doesn't evolution explain

"problem" is in two notes that we have already made for ourselves.

- The world, although polluted, has not yet had time to develop many genetic defects.
- Adam and Eve had other sons and daughters – probably large numbers of them.

So, who was Cain's wife? She must have been his sister.

This answer causes still more problems for some. Doesn't the Bible say that we mustn't marry our sisters? Doesn't the Bible say that we mustn't marry relatives?

Actually, we have to marry relatives. Everyone is a distant cousin of mine, because we are all descended from Adam and Eve. We are not today to marry close relatives.

Today there are lots of genetic defects around. One method of concentrating genetic defects is to marry someone who has similar genetic defects. We can be sure that close relatives have similar genetic defects to ourselves. We see the catastrophic results of such inbreeding in classic situations, such as pedigree dogs and cats, or maybe in the health problems of European Royal Families in the late 19th and early 20th Centuries. It is sensible that the Bible outlaws such liaisons.

However, such liaisons were not outlawed until the time of Moses. In the times of Genesis, no such problems existed. Thus, Jacob goes to his Uncle Laban's house and marries his cousins Rachel and Leah (we'll leave tackling bigamy until another time!). Abraham sends his servant to his family's lands to get a wife for Isaac. Rebecca is a second cousin. Abraham's wife Sarah was actually his half-sister. There is no condemnation of such things, because there was no genetic danger.

It stands to reason, then, that there was no problem with brother and sister being married at the beginning of the world. As soon as a little science is applied to our understanding of the scriptures, we see that they make sense taken literally.

---

our existence?", "How did the different 'races' arise?", and "Does God exist?"

14.5. Descendents of Cain

There is little remarkable about Cain's descendents. A number of issues arise, however.

Cain starts building cities.

We get the first attempt at urbanisation in the Bible. With such a small population, we can perhaps surmise that this is an attempt by Cain to keep some control over the population.

Lamech begins bigamy

The pattern in early Genesis that Jesus approves is that "a man shall leave his father and mother and be joined to his wife, and they shall become one flesh." (Gen 2: 24) The ideal is for one man and one woman – a couple. In this relationship, sexual intercourse is possible. Lamech, the great, great, great grandson of Cain, decides to take two wives. The equal partnership of man and woman is not possible if there are two co-wives. It is significant that Lamech shows an ungodly arrogance in another sense – he belittles God's curse of Cain. "Adah and Zillah, hear my voice; Wives of Lamech, listen to my speech! For I have killed a man for wounding me, Even a young man for hurting me. If Cain shall be avenged sevenfold, then Lamech seventy-sevenfold." Lamech treats what was meant to be a punishment for Cain as a challenge for himself. He is proud about the fact that he has killed someone. Life is cheap to him. It is in the context of his arrogance over the sanctity of life that we see he has no time for morality in personal relationships either. It is this pride that has infected mankind down the ages. Although bigamy is illegal and rare in the UK, biblical bigamy is widespread. There was, after all, no legal marriage ceremony in the time of Genesis. Marriage was accomplished by the act of sexual union. Thus, what we are really talking about with Lamech is not so much bigamy, as promiscuity. Those who have more than one sexual partner are the true spiritual descendents of Lamech, not just those who try to get two marriage certificates.

Industry begins

Along with early urbanisation, we have an early industrial revolution. Three sons of Lamech start three important activities: husbandry of livestock, instrumental music and iron work. Notice that there is no difference between bronze and iron work. There is no bronze age followed by iron age. Tubal-Cain was responsible for starting work in all metals.

14.6. Faith in the Darkness

It is clear that Seth was born after the death of Abel, by Eve's words at his birth. It must be assumed then that Seth was not their third-born. There must have been many other sons and daughters born before Seth, and maybe others afterwards.

Seth's birth prompts a wonderful prophetic outburst from Eve. "God has appointed another seed for me instead of Abel, whom Cain killed". Eve has waited a long time for Seth. She thought that Cain was the promised seed. Perhaps she later thought it might be Abel. What she prayed over the other children, we do not know. Now many, many years later, God grants her the prophetic foresight to know that this one, out of all her sons, was the one through whom God would one day keep His promise. Seth means "appointed", but Eve knows exactly what God has appointed Seth for. The link with Abel is significant. Abel was the "priest", offering the firstborn lamb, as a sin offering, acceptable to God. Seth is the one who takes Abel's place, because Seth's descendent will be the promised Messiah, the seed of the woman, the one who will crush the head of Satan.

For that reason, among Seth and his descendents, we find at last some true worship of God. "Men began to call on the name of the LORD". Throughout the Old Testament, the concept of the "Name of the Lord" is very much analogous with the work of the Holy Spirit in the New

Testament.[38]

Genesis 4 once again emphasises to us that:

- God is a God of power
- God is a loving God, offering salvation
- God's salvation is by the offering of faith, by the shedding of the blood of the lamb – for us, the blood of the perfect Lamb of God, Jesus
- Men and women going their own way fall into deeper and deeper sin
- Even in the midst of such evil, God has His own people who worship Him

---

[38] see, for example, 1 Kings 18:24, Elijah challenging the prophets of Baal - "Then you call on the name of your gods, and I will call on the name of the LORD; and the God who answers by fire, He is God."

15. The Genealogy of Adam

Read Genesis 5

Genesis 5 presents us with a genealogy of ten pre-diluvian patriarchs, from Adam to Noah. There is a danger that these Genesis genealogies can be skipped, as being boring, or of only academic interest. To skip the genealogies, in my view, is to miss out on some precious truths, without which a thorough understanding of Genesis is not really possible.

There are a number of issues to tackle, when looking at this genealogy in Genesis 5. The first, and probably most fundamental, is this: is it complete, or does it contain gaps? It is very important to establish this for our present study, as I am endeavouring to make at least two important theological corollaries of the genealogy being complete.

15.1. Is the Genealogy Complete?

We will begin with a simple explanation. It is a golden rule of Bible interpretation that the simplest interpretation is always the best, unless the context requires otherwise.

> And Adam lived one hundred and thirty years, and begot a son in his own likeness, after his image, and named him Seth. (Gen 5:3)

It is true that the Hebrew word begot can sometimes imply a more distant relationship than the usual father / son. However, its normal meaning is a father / son relationship. So we next need to ask, is there anything in the passage that suggests a generational gap. The answer to that would appear to be "No". Indeed, the existence of ages quoted when the named son is born would seem to suggest that the writer is intending to give us an unbroken timescale.

It is interesting that even Hebrew scholars who do not accept the text as an authentic history, still recognise that the Hebrew grammar implies no gaps in the genealogy. James Barr says:

... probably, so far as I know, there is no professor of Hebrew or Old Testament at any world-class university who does not believe that the writer(s) of Genesis 1–11 intended to convey to their readers the ideas that: ... the figures contained in the Genesis genealogies provided by simple addition a chronology from the beginning of the world up to later stages in the biblical story.[1]

In fact the reason why Barr and others do believe in gaps is not because of the Hebrew, but because of their prior commitment to a great age for the Earth.

Sarfati has gone to great trouble to refute the many spurious objections to the Genesis 5 genealogy being complete, and I would refer readers to his conclusions.[2] He concludes:

A straightforward reading of the biblical genealogies from the reliable Masoretic text shows that Adam was created about 4000 BC and that the Flood occurred around 2500 BC. Contextual, linguistic and historical analyses of the book of Genesis confirm that the chronogenealogies are a complete record with no gaps. Creationists who wish to push back the date of the Flood and creation to fit their geological or archaeological theories have no grounds to do this based on the biblical record. They should rather look to their scientific theories to see where the discrepancies lie.

Moreover, López has shown that the genealogies of Genesis fit well with a correct interpretation of the Sumerian King List.[3] For these reasons, and because of the plain reading of the text, this present study assumes that there are no gaps in the genealogy of Genesis 5.

15.2. The Image of God Tarnished

As a minor digression, notice what Genesis says about Seth in verse 3. "And Adam lived one hundred and thirty years, and begot a son in his own likeness, after his image, and named him Seth." Adam was made in

---

[1] Barr, J., in a letter to David C.C. Watson, 1984, quoted by Sarfati, J. **TJ** 17(3) 2003, p14
[2] Sarfati, J. **TJ** 17(3) 2003, p14ff
[3] López, R.E., **TJ** 12(3) 1998: 347-357

the image of God, but Seth is begotten in the image of Adam. Although Seth is to be the next step in the long line that will lead to the Seed of the Woman, the promised Messiah, Seth was a mere man, born imperfect. It is important for the Bible to note that even the promised line was not created perfect any more. Seth was born in original sin, and is in the image of Adam, who was in the image of God. Seth is not directly in the image of God therefore. The same can be said of us. We are not directly in the image of God, but we are in our parents' image, thus in Adam's image, who was himself in the image of God. The image of God is thus tarnished down the generations, but never fully removed from us.

15.3. The Strange Case of Enoch

What Genesis says about Enoch is tantalising.

And Enoch walked with God; and he was not, for God took him. (verse 24)

That one verse presents us with a fascinating mystery. Enoch did not actually die. The language seems clear. The writer is underlining the fact that Enoch's end was different to the other patriarchs. For all the others, we read about when they died. Enoch, however, was simply taken.

From elsewhere in the Bible, we realise that Enoch was a godly man. His name means teacher. Not only was he a teacher, but he was a prophet. We have one example of his prophecy preserved for us in the Epistle of Jude.

Now Enoch, the seventh from Adam, prophesied about these men also, saying, "Behold, the Lord comes with ten thousands of His saints, to execute judgment on all, to convict all who are ungodly among them of all their ungodly deeds which they have committed in an ungodly way, and of all the harsh things which ungodly sinners have spoken against Him." (Jude 14, 15)

Incidentally, this passage emphasises again the lack of gaps in the genealogy of Genesis 5, because Enoch was the seventh from Adam.

The other passage in the New Testament that speaks about Enoch is in Hebrews 11.

By faith Enoch was taken away so that he did not see death, "and was not found, because God had taken him"; for before he was taken he had this testimony, that he pleased God. But without faith it is impossible to please Him, for he who comes to God must believe that He is, and that He is a rewarder of those who diligently seek Him. (Hebrews 11:5,6)

Enoch preached a gospel of righteousness. Yet this righteousness was by faith, because "without faith it is impossible to please Him". His prophecy, preserved in Jude, is against ungodliness. It is fascinating that even before the Flood a prophet was looking ahead, not to Christ's First coming, but to His Second Coming.

Enoch's unusual translation means that he is one of only two people in the Bible not to have died; the other being Elijah, who was taken up in the famous Chariots of Fire. Is there any significance in this? World renowned creationist Henry Morris suggests that there is. Morris is the only scholar I know to have written excellent commentaries on both Genesis and Revelation. In his commentary on the latter, he suggests that Enoch and Elijah are the two witnesses mentioned in Revelation 11.[4] I am not over-dogmatic on this point, but I have to say that Morris's views make sense to me. This would fit with the Biblical pattern that "it is appointed for men to die once, but after this the judgment" (Hebrews 9:27).

15.4. The Ages of the Patriarchs

A word needs to be said about the great age of the patriarchs.

The fact that the patriarchs lived so long should not really be a surprise to us. We can expect that climactic conditions before the Flood were different to those today. Additionally, we know that the aging process was caused by Adam's sin. The means that God uses to cause this aging seems to be cosmic particles from the Sun. Such particles would not have penetrated before the Flood quite as easily as afterwards. Although I believe that the water canopy of Genesis 1 is in fact at the edge of the universe, rather than the edge of the atmosphere, it seems

---

[4] Morris, H.M., *The Revelation Record*, (Tyndale House, 1983), p193, 194

likely that the water content of the atmosphere would have been greater before the Flood. Neutron bombardment of water molecules causes ^{2}H (deuterium) atoms, of which there is a reasonably stable quantity in water, to become radioactive ^{3}H atoms. These decay by β decay to form ^{3}He atoms. This is not the normal isotope of helium, but it is stable. The present amount of 3He compared to normal ^{4}He can be measured. Since the process of formation is known, we can calculate how much ^{3}He there should be, based on current concentrations of water in the atmosphere. We find that the quantity of ^{3}He is much greater than expected, indicating a much greater concentration of water vapour in the atmosphere at some time in the past.

This would have had a shielding effect, causing less apparent neutron bombardment of the lower atmosphere, thus causing less harmful mutations.

Therefore, in the comparatively short time from Creation to Flood, we would not expect large amounts of mutations to occur, so we could expect great length of life.

15.5. Timing of the Genealogy

Figure 15.1 shows each of the patriarch's birth dates and deaths, assuming no gaps in the genealogy. The vertical line shows the date of the Flood. Note that it happens in the same year that Methuselah dies, and 5 years after Lamech's death.

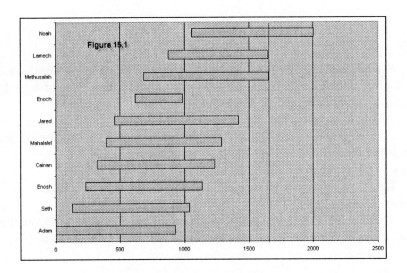

Figure 15.2 magnifies the relevant section.

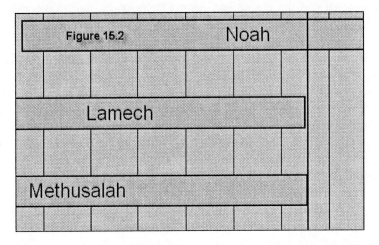

None of the patriarchs before Noah were alive at the time of the Flood, but Methuselah had only just died. This fact has great significance when compared with the meaning of the names given below.

15.6. The Meaning of the Names

We are probably by now used to the idea that Hebrew names have a meaning. However, the meaning of the names of the ten patriarchs provides a very interesting insight into the prediluvian world.[5]

Adam, as we have already seen, means Man.

Seth means appointed. Eve gave this name, to show her faith in the fact that God would deliver the promised Messiah though the appointed son.

Enosh means mortal. This emphasises once again that man is now mortal, because of sin.

Kenan means sorrow. The existence of sin causes sorrow. Imagine the sorrow of Adam and Eve at the death of their son, Abel. Death brings such sorrow that even Jesus was caused to weep at the tomb of his friend Lazarus.[6]

Mahalalel means "the God who is to be praised". We have noted earlier how all was not gloom and doom. There was a start to worship of the Lord God. Mahalalel's name emphasises the existence of those who want to worship God in faith.

Jared means "shall come down". This is one of the more puzzling names, until we put them all together below.

Enoch means "teaching". It seems that Enoch was a teacher and prophet.

Methuselah means "his death shall bring". We will see that there are two reasons for this. The first is that the Flood came the very year that Methuselah died. His death is prophetic, pointing to the way of salvation, and warning against doubt.

Lamech means "despairing". It is perhaps significant that he died before he could see the salvation caused by the Flood. He was also a prophet, prophesying that Noah would "comfort us concerning our work and the toil of our hands, because of the ground which the LORD has cursed." This is significant as well, because Noah means rest, or comfort.

There is a passage of the Bible that contains all these names one after

---

[5] Meanings based on McIntosh, A. *Genesis for today*, (DayOne: 1997), p127
[6] John 11:35

the other. It is 1 Chronicles 1:1-3 "Adam, Seth, Enosh, Cainan, Mahalalel, Jared, Enoch, Methuselah, Lamech, Noah". Now that we know the meanings, this passage can be read as follows:

Man is appointed mortal sorrow, but the God who is to be praised shall come down, teaching that His death shall bring the despairing rest.

This is remarkable that in the very names of the ten patriarchs from before the Flood, through whose line God was to send the Messiah, should spell out a dramatic statement of the Gospel. This can surely be no coincidence. It is one of the exciting things about studying Genesis that we see over and over again that it is foundational to the understanding of all the Bible. God gave us hope right from the very beginning. Even in the midst of the dreadful evil before the Flood, God would not leave us without a way of salvation. That wonderful work of salvation will be seen more clearly, as we study what God did when He destroyed the world in a Flood.

16. Before the Flood

Read Genesis 6

Too many Christians today do not understand the central fundamental importance of the Flood to our knowledge of theology. The Answers in Genesis organisation have produced a useful mnemonic which shows the place of the Flood in our history. They refer to the Seven C's of History – Creation, Corruption, Catastrophe, Confusion, Christ, Cross, Consummation. Just as the sin of Adam followed creation, and his failure as our first representative, so the Catastrophe – the Flood – follows by the judgment of God as a type of the judgment to come at the end of all things.

The problem is that so many Christians do not even believe that the Flood was a worldwide catastrophic event. Thus its central importance to the history of the world is lost, as it becomes a legend of a local Flood in a tribal mythology.

It is the writer's contention in this book that the Flood was global in extent. Such a global Flood would be expected to have left major geological evidence, and it is also suggested here that much of the earth's geology has come about as a direct or indirect result of the Flood. It is furthermore suggested that the Flood is typical of the judgment to come (2 Peter 3) and anti-typical of baptism (1 Peter 3).

16.1. Sons of God and Daughters of Men

The use of these two terms has caused much controversy over the ages. Daughters of men should not cause us any confusion – these are as described; the daughters of ordinary people. So why is there a distinction between daughters of men and sons of God?

There are some who have suggested that the sons of God were angelic beings – probably fallen angels. Morris makes this point.[1] He looks at

---

[1] Morris, H.M., *The Genesis Record*, (Baker Book House, 1976), p165

other occurrences of the phrase *bene elohim*, which occurs in 6:1 and 6:4. He shows that this phrase also occurs in Job three times – Job 1:6, 2:1 and 38:7. In each of these three occasions, angelic beings seem to be described.

Ham, Sarfati and Weiland, on the other hand, show that similar phrases are used elsewhere in scripture.[2]

While acknowledging that I am not entirely sure on this issue, I am uncomfortable with Morris's explanation of angelic beings. Such beings would seem elsewhere in the Bible to be incapable of reproducing. If they were able to reproduce, then there would be a race of angelic beings, and the possibility of an angelic saviour would seem to be available. As it is, there is no angelic saviour – there is no salvation for the fallen angels. They are separate creations and representative only of themselves. Jesus can be our Representative and Saviour, because Adam was our failed representative in the Garden.

It would seem more likely to this writer that the phrase "sons of God" refers to the spiritual state of these people.

Adam was directly created by God. In Gen 5:1 we are reminded that Adam was made in the likeness of God. In Gen 5:3 we read that Seth was born in the likeness of Adam. If Adam was in the likeness of God, then there is an extent to which Seth was also in the likeness of God. It could be that the phrase refers to the imperfection of human beings, yet we do not read of Cain or any other descendents being in the likeness of Adam. We know that Seth was an important part of the liner of descent, the seed of the woman, that was to end at the birth of Jesus Christ. This important position of Seth is emphasised in the last two verses of chapter 4.

> And Adam knew his wife again, and she bore a son and named him Seth, "For God has appointed another seed for me instead of Abel, whom Cain killed." And as for Seth, to him also a son was born; and he named him Enosh. Then men began to call on the name of the LORD. (Gen 4:25,26)

This calling on the name of the LORD would appear to imply worship. Thus it would seem likely that the sons of God referred to in 5:2 are those who worship the LORD.

---

[2] Ham, K., Sarfati, J., Wieland, C., *The Answers Book*, (Master Books:2000), p143

If that is the case, then the contrast being drawn between sons of God and daughters of men must be a spiritual contrast. It can be assumed that these daughters of men are not worshippers of the LORD – possibly daughters of Cain. A key phrase suggested here, which demonstrates why such unions should not have happened, is that "they took wives for themselves of all whom they chose."

Throughout history, God has been clear that His people are not to take wives from whom they chose. The Israelites were told later that they were not to marry outside Israel. This was not racist – witness the approval of the marriage of Ruth and Boaz. This latter marriage shows that the concern was for faith.

When Abraham was looking for a wife for Isaac, he sent his servant off, saying to him "I will make you swear by the LORD, the God of heaven and the God of the earth, that you will not take a wife for my son from the daughters of the Canaanites, among whom I dwell." (Gen 24:3)

In the New Testament, we are urged "Do not be unequally yoked together with unbelievers. For what fellowship has righteousness with lawlessness? And what communion has light with darkness?" (2 Corinthians 6:14)

It is God's will that He be part of the most precious and intimate human relationship possible – that of husband and wife. So throughout the Bible it has always been necessary that people of faith should marry only other people of faith.

In Gen 6:2 it seems that we have people of faith marrying those who do not share that faith – who are outside of the worship of God. Thus sin is creeping in even into the midst of God's people in this world before the Flood.

16.2. The Warning of Judgment

The words of God in this chapter count as some of the most devastating and disturbing words of God anywhere in the Bible.

And the LORD said, "My Spirit shall not strive with man forever, for he is indeed flesh; yet his days shall be one hundred and twenty years." (Gen 6:3)

The result of the sinfulness of mankind is a striving with God. There is either peace with God or striving with God.

People may think that they govern themselves. They do not. There is a limit to how far God can be "abused" by people. In Galatians 6:7 we read: "Do not be deceived, God is not mocked; for whatever a man sows, that he will also reap." There is only so far that God will be pushed. It might seem that those without God succeed in life, but there is always a limit. Those who try to mock God learn eventually that it is He who has the last laugh.

> He who sits in the heavens shall laugh; The Lord shall hold them in derision. Then He shall speak to them in His wrath, And distress them in His deep displeasure (Psalm 2:4,5)

The sin of mankind before the Flood was dreadful. We possibly cannot imagine how depraved the world had got – though our own world is probably nearly as bad, if not worse.

> Then the LORD saw that the wickedness of man was great in the earth, and that every intent of the thoughts of his heart was only evil continually. And the LORD was sorry that He had made man on the earth, and He was grieved in His heart. So the LORD said, "I will destroy man whom I have created from the face of the earth, both man and beast, creeping thing and birds of the air, for I am sorry that I have made them." (Gen 6:5-7)

The wickedness was so bad that it had infected God's own people. Although we know that there was the line of descent, with godly men such as Enoch, we can also surmise that other descendents of Seth were now as evil as descendents of Cain. No longer were there thoughts of calling on the name of the LORD – rather "every intent of the thoughts of his heart was only evil continually". It is verse 6 that contains the words I find most disturbing: "And the LORD was sorry that He had made man on the earth, and He was grieved in His heart." That the LORD regretted creating mankind, and that mankind grieved Him, is most dreadful. Is that how God feels today, as He looks over this world?

Because God had chosen to end the world by Flood, this also required the destruction of land animals and birds. Since god had made them, it was up to Him determine their fate. It is likely that, though we cannot speak of animals as sinners, nevertheless something of the corruption of the mankind had polluted land animals and birds.

God's regret, as He looked over the world, would always be God's attitude, but for the fact that God is also Love personified.

But Noah found grace in the eyes of the LORD.

What was it that saved Noah? It was grace, just as it is today. The Apostle Paul says "For by grace you have been saved through faith, and that not of yourselves; it is the gift of God, not of works, lest anyone should boast." (Ephesians 2:8,9) No one is saved by the good works that they do themselves. If this were a treatise on saving faith, then I could expand on this over and over. Those of you who are saved know the references: "All our righteousnesses are like filthy rags" (Isaiah 64:6). For now, suffice it to say that Noah was a man saved by the Gospel of Jesus Christ, before Jesus was born into history, before God had separated his chosen people Israel, before even the destruction of the world in the Flood.

In the Bible, the word grace is synonymous with the word favour. A favour is something done when there is no means of repayment. We hear children in the playground asking "Will you do me a favour?" If a favour is done, there is no payment. I know that I needed a favour from God. I couldn't save myself. God did me a favour. He saved me, by sending His Son Jesus Christ to die for me. Even the faith I have to believe this came from God Himself.

By faith Noah, being divinely warned of things not yet seen, moved with godly fear, prepared an ark for the saving of his household, by which he condemned the world and became heir of the righteousness which is according to faith. (Hebrews 11:7)

It was faith that enabled Noah to do what he did. It is true that he was warned by God – "his days shall be one hundred and twenty years" (v3) – but Noah had never seen a Flood. Such an event had never happened before. He built the Ark because of faith. That is why the writer of

Hebrews reminds us:

> Now faith is the substance of things hoped for, the evidence of things not seen. (Hebrews 11:1)

> But without faith it is impossible to please Him, for he who comes to God must believe that He is, and that He is a rewarder of those who diligently seek Him. (Hebrews 11:6)

There is always an answer to the wickedness of the world. It is through faith in Him who can save us. Here in Genesis 6, before the Flood, we learn yet again that God has always been the same; God the Judge and God the Saviour, the God of Wrath against sin and sinners, and the God of Love who loves sinners. Like Christians today, Noah was saved, not because of anything he had done, but because of the grace of God, through his faith in God.

> This is the genealogy of Noah. Noah was a just man, perfect in his generations. Noah walked with God. (Gen 6:9)

In the early chapters of Genesis, the Flood was God's means of destroying the world. Thus for us the Flood is a type of the judgment to come. Yet even as God planned to destroy the world, He also planned a way of salvation, for those who found grace in the eyes of the LORD.

16.3. Heroes and Giants

> There were giants on the earth in those days, and also afterward, when the sons of God came in to the daughters of men and they bore children to them. Those were the mighty men who were of old, men of renown. (Gen 6:4)

Almost parenthetically, it is worth discussing verse 4. What is meant by the giants and the heroes (mighty men)?

It has been assumed by some that the giants were the offspring of the liaisons between the sons of God and the daughters of men. This is partly because of the uncertainty about the translation of the term nephilim. The

NIV leaves the word untranslated, and capitalises the first letter, giving an impression that this was an unusual human tribe. Some have even suggested that the Nephilim could be extra-terrestrial beings – a view that needn't detain us here, though Ham, Sarfati and Wieland have discussed this at length in the Answers Book.[3]

There are two reasons why I don't accept that these giants are the offspring of the sons of God and the daughters of men:

- As stated above, I don't accept that the sons of God mentioned in this chapter are angelic beings
- The syntax suggests that there were giants on the earth **before** the liaisons between the sons of God and daughters of men.

One of the purposes of this work has been to demonstrate the harmony between genuine science, and the accounts in the Bible. Therefore I will suggest a scientific answer to what the giants may have been. I will have to emphasise, however, that this section of the work is conjecture on my part.

If the word nephilim can be correctly translated as giants, then there is no reason to suppose it refers only to humans. It could simply be referring to the sizes of some animals and plants before the Flood.

Fossils of creatures which are known today often demonstrate giantism. Visit any natural history museum, and you will see such fossils. Maybe there will be giant dragonflies, with metre wingspans, or giant beetles. Vertebrates are not unknown in giant forms. What is being suggested here is a reminder that creatures before the Flood could have been larger than after the Flood.

As we have seen earlier, there would certainly have been less genetic mutations before the Flood. We have also seen that human ages before the Flood were greater than those after. These ages could have been reflected in the ages of animals, as well. If these longer-lived animals kept growing for a longer time than their contemporary counterparts, then they could easily have grown larger than today's creatures.

All in all, the pre-diluvian world was a strange and wonderful place. My suggestion is also that many of the characters of mythology, though

---

[3] Ham, K., Sarfati, J., Wieland, C., *The Answers Book*, (Master Books:2000), p141

their stories have no doubt been exaggerated, may have had real life antecedents amongst the heroes of the world before the Flood.

Mythology is very important to those studying the Flood. Many accounts have been compiled of other Flood legends from around the world. Some of these other Flood legends are fairly well known – such as that in the Epic of Gilgamesh. Others are less familiar, such as accounts by Australian Aborigines. Some have suggested that the Bible account is copied from accounts such as Gilgamesh. However, the uncertainties in dating are such that it is equally possible – and likely, in my mind – for Gilgamesh to have been based on the Bible account. But even if Gilgamesh were written earlier, that would not invalidate the reality of the biblical Flood. Gilgamesh would still have been written long after the Flood – long enough for the details to have got corrupted.

The study of other Flood legends, and the light they shed on the real Flood, is a fascinating study, and, in my mind, worthy of a book all by itself.

16.4. God's Blueprint for the Ark

So many pictures of the Ark give a false picture. We often see children's story books of a boat overloaded with animals. We should not be surprised at such falsehoods, but nor should we, as Christians, encourage them. I am disturbed whenever I see Christian Sunday School materials, with illustrations of such a toy-type Ark.

The truth is that the Ark was thoroughly suited to its task. The Bible is so clear on how the Ark was built, that it would be possible, were someone inclined, to reproduce the Ark.

Although many have said that the Bible is not a science text book, the second half of Genesis 6 looks pretty much like it. As others have said, I am glad that the Bible is not a science text book. Science text books change every year or so, as new discoveries are made, whereas the Bible is always true. However, one aspect of scientific methodology requires that experiments should be reproducible. So much information about the Ark has been given, that many people have made models, or carried out experiments, and determined that the Ark would work precisely as it was designed to do.

This drawing, from the Flood Film web site (www.floodfilm.com) illustrates how the Ark would need to withstand tremendous tidal forces. It turns out, from hydrodynamic experiments, that the best shape to withstand such a buffeting is, in fact, the exact shape of the Ark.

The verses which speak of the measurements of the Ark almost don't need any commentary. In any case, the scientific details have been covered in far greater detail than I could ever manage by John Woodmorappe.[4] Let us just examine a few salient points here, and I will leave the reader to fill in the gaps by reading Woodmorappe's book.

> And Noah begot three sons: Shem, Ham, and Japheth. The earth also was corrupt before God, and the earth was filled with violence. So God looked upon the earth, and indeed it was corrupt; for all flesh had corrupted their way on the earth. And God said to Noah, "The end of all flesh has come before Me, for the earth is filled with violence through them; and behold, I will destroy them with the earth. (Genesis 6:10-13)

The impression given in other genealogies is that the patriarchs may

---

[4] Woodmorappe, J., *Noah's Ark: A Feasibility Study*, (ICR:1996)

have had many sons, but only the important one, through whom Christ was descended, is mentioned. In this case, three sons are mentioned.

I think it is perfectly possible that Noah had other sons. However, these three are mentioned, because they are the only ones saved with Noah on the Ark. Thus, through these sons, all nations of the world are descended.

As we prepare for God's instructions to Noah, we are reminded once again of the sin and corruption on the earth. It is noteworthy that the Bible speaks of the Earth being filled with violence. Sin and violence accompany one another. This pre-diluvian world was clearly a dangerous place to live.

The significant point about the verses just quoted is that God chooses to reveal His plans in advance to Noah. Noah is not just told to build an Ark. He is told **why** he must build an Ark. This gives Noah the opportunity, in his day to day life, to explain this point to any who would listen. We know he was likely to do this, because he was described by Peter, in 2 Peter 2:5, as a "preacher of righteousness".

Some have said that a wooden ship would get waterlogged. It is fortunate, then, that the Ark was coated in pitch, a point we will return to shortly. But it is now known that there were other giant ships in the ancient world. Ships approaching the Ark in size were not as unknown as once thought.

Woodmorappe has spent a long time with the measurements. The difficulty with the measurements is to know what length a cubit is. It appears that it could be anything between 42 and 57 cm. In order to demonstrate the practicability of the Ark, Woodmorappe has used the shortest cubit in his measurements, though an average cubit of 48cm is more likely.

Notice that the Ark is made with three floors, and a "window" opening at the top, which would allow circulation of air. The next supposed problem thrown at creationists is the suggestion that Noah would never have been able to fit the millions of species onto the Ark. This point is invalid. We have already discussed how the Bible speaks of *kinds* rather than *species* – a more modern word. The baraminologists are suggesting that the total number of kinds is, in fact, much less – maybe as little as 16000. Remember also that it is only kinds of land animals and birds that are necessary, plus the food and bedding they might need. Again, critics ask about dinosaurs. However, we have already discussed giantism. Maybe the natural size of many of these giants was less than the large fossils, but even if it were not, it is well established that the vast majority of dinosaurs were small. Maybe the really large saurupods, such as Brachiosaurus, Apatosaurus and Diplodocus were all part of the same baramin.

Now let's revisit the fact that the Ark was covered in pitch. This would clearly make the Ark watertight.

The pitch creates a problem to some creationists. Pitch is usually obtained from petrochemical sources. Petroleum is assumed by creationists to have been formed during the flood, so how could pitch be used to coat the Ark?

There are two main explanations. The word oil can also refer to vegetable oil. Perhaps vegetable grease could be used as a form of pitch. Another suggestion, however, which Woodmorappe supports, suggests that some petroleum could be of non-organic origin. This suggestion is, in fact, supported by a number of non-Christian, non-creationist geologists as well.

It causes this writer no problem to imagine that some hydrocarbon-based greasy, hydrophobic substance could have been used to coat the wood of the Ark, in the same way that modern, petrochemical pitch is used today, whether the pre-diluvian pitch was petrochemical in origin or not.

The interesting thing about the pitch is that the Hebrew word used is *kopher*. This is similar to the Hebrew word for cover, and implies a covering. What is special about this word for covering, however, is that it is translated elsewhere in the Bible as *atonement*. The atoning pitch covering the Ark kept the occupants safe from the judgment of water, just as the atoning blood of Jesus, the perfect Lamb of God, keeps out the fires of God's judgment to come.

The final point to notice from Genesis 6 is that the whole rescue mission was to repopulate the world, with food and a complete environment, for the sake of the people being saved through the Ark, and their descendents. That it was done for the sake of the people on the Ark is shown by the fact that God establishes a covenant with Noah. Because of Noah's faith, and the grace of God, Noah is to share in a covenant with God. This covenant will save Noah and his family, yet the whole of the bargaining and the work is from God Himself. That is the nature of our one-sided covenant through Jesus. We cannot save ourselves, as

Noah could not save himself. We need the atoning blood of Jesus to cover us, as Noah needed the atoning pitch to cover. We are saved by the death of Jesus, just as Noah was saved by the Ark.

> But when the kindness and the love of God our Saviour toward man appeared, not by works of righteousness which we have done, but according to His mercy He saved us, through the washing of regeneration and renewing of the Holy Spirit, whom He poured out on us abundantly through Jesus Christ our Saviour, that having been justified by His grace we should become heirs according to the hope of eternal life. (Titus 3:4-7)

Notice Noah's reaction.

Thus Noah did; according to all that God commanded him, so he did.

We should expect nothing else. These, after all, are the words of Jesus.

> He who has My commandments and keeps them, it is he who loves Me. And he who loves Me will be loved by My Father, and I will love him and manifest Myself to him. (John 14:21)

Noah demonstrated his faith in God by his actions.

17. The Flood Begins

Read Genesis 7

17.1. Into Noah's Ark

Then the LORD said to Noah, "Come into the ark, you and all your household, because I have seen that you are righteous before Me in this generation."

In the subheading above, I have deliberately called the Ark Noah's Ark, because that is the popular name for it. In fact, the Ark was made at God's command, following God's instructions. It was filled with animals according to God's instructions. As we will see, Noah had no way even of closing the door or of steering the Ark. He was in no way the captain of a ship. Rather than calling the Ark Noah's Ark, we ought more properly to call it God's Ark. It was God's Ark for the salvation of mankind.

Verse 1 gives us a clear reason for Noah and his family being saved from the Flood. It was because God saw that Noah was righteous before Him. As discussed earlier, this righteousness came not from Noah himself, but because of the grace of God.

"You shall take with you seven each of every clean animal, a male and his female; two each of animals that are unclean, a male and his female; also seven each of birds of the air, male and female, to keep the species alive on the face of all the earth."

The well known children's song suggests that the animals went in two by two. As we see from this verse, this is not entirely correct.

God was intending to repopulate the Earth. This very command gives the lie to the view that the Flood was only going to be a local affair. If the Flood was local in scope, what purpose would there be in saving all of these animals? If God wanted to repopulate just a local area, the animals could have been brought in from beyond the locality. Yet God states clearly that he wants "to keep the species alive on the face of all the Earth.

A word about the translation at this point: The NKJV refers to "the species". This is not a correct translation, as *species* is a modern word, referring to a grouping, within which there can be breeding, but outside of which breeding will be difficult of not impossible. Compare the translations of NKJV, NIV and KJV.

NKJV ...to keep the species alive on the face of all the earth.
NIV ...to keep their various kinds alive throughout the earth.
KJV ...to keep seed alive upon the face of all the earth.

In this case, I prefer the NIV. The word translated as *kinds* has been used in the early chapters of Genesis, and has been discussed at length there. It refers to a broader grouping than species. The KJV uses *seed*, which is acceptable, but ought to have used *kind* as that was the word used earlier. On the other hand, I prefer the ending of the sentence in the KJV and NKJV – "the face of all the earth" – as this is emphasising the totality of the destruction God was about to bring.

One of the principle criticisms of the Genesis account hinges on this verse. The question raised is this: "How did Noah get all those animals on to the Ark?" Ham *et al* summarise these questions in The Answers Book[1]. They pose the questions "What animals did Noah take onto the ark? Where did they store all the food? How could the ark be big enough? What about all the animal wastes?"

As The Answers Book goes on to show, there are a number of false presumptions in these questions. The first false presumption is that two of every *species* had to be taken on to the Ark. This is not the case. There would only be a need for two of every *kind*. Thus there didn't need to be two lions, two tigers, two cheetahs etc. Just two cats, or rather animals of the cat baramin would suffice. Indeed, it is almost certain that the species mentioned would not have existed before the Flood, but would all have developed from the pair of cat-kind creatures after the Flood, by speciation. As we have observed earlier, creationists believe in speciation and development within the baramins.

---

[1] Ham, K., Sarfati, J., Wieland, C., *The Answers Book*, (Master Books:2000)

Also note that, contrary to popular opinion, Noah was not taking every kind of animal. Genesis 6:19, 20 refers to Noah taking of every kind of flesh, birds and creeping things. The NIV has *living things* at this point. The word used is, in fact, nephesh, which we saw refers to the animals that have blood in them – what we might term the higher animals. We have previously divided animals into nephesh and non-nephesh. The division goes further, because Noah is instructed to take land animals, not sea animals. There was no requirement to take fish or aquatic mammals, as they would not be destroyed by the Flood. There was no requirement to take non-nephesh kinds, such as insects. Writers such as Woodmorappe[2] have shown that there are possible mechanisms for the survival of insects and other non-nephesh kinds, by vegetation rafts.

These verses are the first occasion, on which we are given a differentiation between clean and unclean animals. Noah is told to take more clean animals, presumably to enable sacrifices after the Flood, because he and his family were not given leave to eat animals until after the Flood.

> For after seven more days I will cause it to rain on the earth forty days and forty nights, and I will destroy from the face of the earth all living things that I have made.

Even at this late stage, God still delays His destruction of the Earth by seven days. God gave mankind 120 years to change their ways. Now, 120 years later, He is prepared to wait seven more days. This shows yet again the love and long-suffering of God. As He says in the prophecy of Ezekiel

> 'As I live,' says the Lord GOD, 'I have no pleasure in the death of the wicked, but that the wicked turn from his way and live. Turn, turn from your evil ways! For why should you die, O house of Israel?' (Ez 33:11)

God has given, God gives and God will give every opportunity for the reluctant sinner to repent and be saved. God has gone the extra mile. But in the case of Noah's Flood not one extra person came to be saved. Yet

---

[2] Woodmorappe, J., *Noah's Ark: A Feasibility Study*, (ICR:1996)

God's justice is seen to be just and loving.

Another reason for the delay of seven days must be to do with the number seven. Seven days are one week, the only time scale we use that is not astronomical in nature. Once again, God is reminding us that He made the world in seven days. This seven day delay could be a source of comfort to Noah and His family, reminding them that the God who made the world in six days could remake everything after the Flood.

17.2. Noah on the Ark

And Noah did according to all that the LORD commanded him. Noah was six hundred years old when the floodwaters were on the earth.

As the Flood was about to start, we are reminded of why Noah and his family are about to be saved. Noah has found favour in the eyes of the LORD, and demonstrates his faith in the LORD by his obedience.

So Noah, with his sons, his wife, and his sons' wives, went into the ark because of the waters of the flood. Of clean animals, of animals that are unclean, of birds, and of everything that creeps on the earth, two by two they went into the ark to Noah, male and female, as God had commanded Noah. And it came to pass after seven days that the waters of the flood were on the earth.

God kept His part of the bargain completely. When God promises punishment, He may delay, as He did in this case, but He does what He says.

The punishments God gives teach us two things: first that God will always keep His promises, and second that God prefers to bless than to punish. He punishes when needs must, and will keep to His word. But He is swifter to fulfil his promises of blessing. The delays in His fulfilment of promises to punish are yet another sign of His grace.

In the six hundredth year of Noah's life, in the second month, the seventeenth day of the month, on that day all the fountains of the great deep were broken up, and the windows of heaven were opened. And the rain was on the earth forty days and forty nights.

These two short verses tell us something about the mechanism required for the Flood to happen.

We need to recap some of the points made earlier. In our studies of Genesis 2, we saw that the pre-diluvian hydrological cycle was different from that of today. It is my suspicion that there was no rain before the Flood. This would be due to an absence of dust in the atmosphere, around which raindrops could coalesce.

Some creationists used to suggest that there a canopy of water vapour around the atmosphere. They point to the separation of waters above and below the firmament, in support of this theory. However, there are severe problems with the canopy theory. First, the water canopy would cause the heat and pressure at the Earth's surface to be too great for life as we know it. Second, there would still be insufficient water to account for the Flood. Third, we have already speculated that the separation of water might be due to a water layer outside the current bounds of the universe, rather than merely above the atmosphere. Fourth, we see here in Genesis 7 that the Flood waters continued to rise, even after the forty days of rain. There is no doubt that there was much rain in the Flood. However, the bulk of the Flood waters must have come from another source.

We have already postulated the idea of vast underground flows of water – the fountains of the deep. If these fountains existed, then they must have been completely destroyed. Genesis 7:11 suggests that these fountains were indeed a major source of Flood water. In order to break this immense pre-diluvian hydrology, there must have been substantial seismic and volcanic events for the first time in Earth's history. These would have broken open these fountains, and produced the dust required for raindrops to form. This first ever rain would be substantial. Genesis describes it as "the windows of heaven" being opened.

It is worth emphasising that the Flood was a worldwide event. Such a major catastrophe would have completely reshaped the Earth's crust. This would enable the huge movements of the crust that we expect after the Flood.

On the very same day Noah and Noah's sons, Shem, Ham, and Japheth, and Noah's wife and the three wives of his sons with them, entered the ark – they and every beast after its kind, all cattle after their kind, every creeping thing that creeps on the earth after its kind, and every bird after its

114

kind, every bird of every sort. And they went into the ark to Noah, two by two, of all flesh in which is the breath of life. So those that entered, male and female of all flesh, went in as God had commanded him; and the LORD shut him in.

There is a lot of repetition in this account of the Flood. Wherever there is repetition, it is usually the case that God is trying to get an important lesson home – usually one of emphasising the facts. It is this very repetition that aids us in our interpretation of these verses. Indeed, no interpretation is necessary. Even liberal scholars agree that the writer of this passage must have been trying to convey that the sequence of events was exactly as written. We need to underline these points:

- There were just 8 people saved, because of the faith of Noah.
- Noah's three sons were Shem, Ham and Japheth, the ancestors of all races of people.
- On the ark were beasts, cattle, creeping things and birds. This would seem to include at least all land based vertebrates.
- Note that the animals enter two by two, each after its *kind* or baramin. This does not mean that two of every species was saved.
- The animals were male and female, emphasising again the importance of the two genders.
- The animals came to Noah – he did not have to collect them.

Notice also that the door of the Ark had to be closed from the outside. "The LORD shut him in". If the door had not been shut, Noah and his family would have drowned. God made sure the door was closed.

The ark is very much a type of Christ. Thus we can say that our salvation is from God. We are not capable of saving ourselves. We need to know that God has closed the door from the outside.

17.3. During the Flood

Now the flood was on the earth forty days. The waters increased and lifted up the ark, and it rose high above the earth. The waters prevailed and greatly increased on the earth, and the ark moved about on the surface of the waters. And the waters prevailed exceedingly on the earth, and all the high hills under the whole heaven were covered. The waters prevailed fifteen cubits upward, and the mountains were covered.

The context of this section seems to suggest that the water continued to increase somewhat after the forty days of rain: "The waters prevailed and greatly increased". This would also suggest an alternative to the rain as the major source of Flood water. This alternative is the source of water provided by the fountains of the deep.

This passage gives the lie to the belief that the Flood was only a local event. If it were only a local event, we would not read about the ark moving about, nor about the water prevailing exceedingly on the earth, nor about the high hills being covered.

In 1973, the TV personality and world famous diver, Jacques Cousteau, said:

Were the crust of Earth to be leveled-with great mountain ranges like the Himalayas and ocean abysses like the Mariana Trench evened out-no land at all would show above the surface of the sea. Earth would be covered by a uniform sheet of water-more than 10,000 feet deep! So overwhelming the ocean seems to be.[3]

This shows that there is plenty of water today for there to have been a worldwide Flood. We do not require 10000 feet of water – just fifteen cubits.

One ironic development is that the very scientists, who claim that a worldwide Flood on the Earth is impossible, postulate a global flood on Mars.[4] It seems completely reasonable to such scientists that Mars, a world with very little water, was once completely covered in water, whereas the Earth, a world which is today two-thirds covered by water, could never have been completely covered by water. Attitudes like this are part of the "wilful forgetfulness" of those, who want to deny the

[3] Cousteau, J., *The Ocean World of Jacques Cousteau - Oasis In Space*, Angus & Robertson (U.K.) Ltd. London, England, p.17, 1973

[4] Reuters, Mars Calamity May have Created Conditions for Life. *New York Times*, 16 March, 2001

existence or work of God.[5]

Even forty years ago, Whitcomb and Morris were suggesting that the Flood water was still with us, comprising the present oceans.[6] We need to assume, therefore, that the current ocean depths are deeper than they were before the Flood and the mountain heights are higher than before the Flood. This fits with what we read in the Bible. Psalm 104:8 (RSV) says "The mountains rose, the valleys sank down to the place which thou didst appoint for them." The difficulty in reading Psalm 104:8 is in working out what the subject of the sentence is. The NIV, AV and NKJV have the waters rising up. However, the RSV and NAS have the mountains going up and valleys going down. Charles Taylor shows that this is the natural meaning of the Psalm. "The Septuagint (LXX), a Greek translation done about 250 B.C., Luther's German translation, which pre-dates the KJV, and French and Italian translations all agree."[7]

The Bibliography contains a number of books, which give further information on the mechanisms and implications of belief in a literal worldwide Flood. These include technical scientific articles from CEN Technical Journal, and Creation Research Society Quarterly, as well popular style books such as:

- The Genesis Flood, by Whitcomb and Morris
- The Genesis Record, by H.M. Morris
- The Young Earth, by John D. Morris
- Noah's Ark: A Feasibility Study, by J. Woodmorappe

Indeed, this whole area is one of the most fruitful for creation scientists, so the reader, who wants to study beyond the brief summaries I have made, will find no shortage of material.

And all flesh died that moved on the earth: birds and cattle and beasts and every creeping thing that creeps on the earth, and every man. All in whose nostrils was the breath of the spirit of life, all that was on the dry land, died.

---

[5] 2 Peter 3:5

[6] Whitcomb, J.C. and Morris, H.M., *The Genesis Flood*, (Baker: 1961), p125-125

[7] Taylor, C.V., *Did the Mountains Really Rise According to Psalm 104:8?*, CEN TJ 12 (3) 312-313, 1998

So He destroyed all living things which were on the face of the ground: both man and cattle, creeping thing and bird of the air. They were destroyed from the earth. Only Noah and those who were with him in the ark remained alive. And the waters prevailed on the earth one hundred and fifty days.

These verses show the completeness if God's destruction of the Earth. Once more, it is being emphasised to us that the Flood was a global event. "All flesh... all in whose nostrils was the breath of the spirit of life, all that was on the dry land, died". Thus the Flood was a spiritual event. All *nephesh* life forms had to die, as symbolic of the purging of the sin of the world.

It is instructive to note what did not die. Animals that were not *nephesh* did not die. These are the animals with their life-blood in them – i.e. *flesh*. Animals that do not breathe through nostrils into lungs did not die. This includes insects. The Bible is clear that they must have survived. We can only surmise how, though many have suggested that they could have lodged in vegetation mats. A number of possible explanations are suggested by Batten and Sarfati.[8]

Amphibians, also, though having lungs, could have survived the Flood, as they absorb oxygen through their skin. Certainly amphibian larvae would survive as easily as fish.

Finally, even nephesh life that breathes through its nostrils would survive if it was not included in "all that was on the dry land". So whales, dolphins and other marine mammals, and, possibly, marine reptiles, such as ichthyosaur, would survive.

But God was preserving a remnant, through the ark, to repopulate the world.

---

[8] Batten, D. and Sarfati, J. *How did fish and plants survive the Genesis Flood?*, http://www.answersingenesis.org/docs/444.asp

18. The Flood Recedes

Read Genesis 8

In Genesis 7, we learned that it rained for forty days. We also learned that the waters prevailed or continued to rise for a further period of 150 days. This was due to sources of water from the fountains of the deep.

18.1 Floodwaters stop

After this period of time, we find that the waters at last start to recede. This is not part of some natural cycle. The reason given is clear.

> Then God remembered Noah, and every living thing, and all the animals that were with him in the ark. And God made a wind to pass over the earth, and the waters subsided. The fountains of the deep and the windows of heaven were also stopped, and the rain from heaven was restrained. And the waters receded continually from the earth. At the end of the hundred and fifty days the waters decreased.

The waters receded to allow the Earth to recover, because "God remembered Noah". This world that was originally created for the benefit of mankind, is now once again re-created for the benefit of Noah and his descendents.

There is no necessity to assume that the wind was a strong wind, blowing water away. Instead, the existence of the wind confirms that there is now a differential in air pressure, enabling wind to move from high to low pressure. It is at this point, however, that God blocks up the sources of water for the Flood, and then Noah and his family were into a waiting game, waiting for the waters to recede.

The Hebrew word used for the wind is *ruach*. Elsewhere, this word is also used for Spirit. Morris observes that it could be implied that the Spirit of God is once more hovering over the waters, as He did at creation.[1]

18.2 Land Appears

Then the ark rested in the seventh month, the seventeenth day of the month, on the mountains of Ararat. And the waters decreased continually until the tenth month. In the tenth month, on the first day of the month, the tops of the mountains were seen.

The dreadful events of the Flood must have started enormous geological changes in the crust. Many creation geologists have pointed to these events as the possible beginning of plate tectonics.

Certainly there must have been much activity at this stage. Mountains were being pushed up, and depths and trenches were lowering, so that the water was finding new levels. At this point, we are told that mountains can be seen. Since Noah and his family are the only people left alive, it must be them who see the mountains. It would be natural for them to be looking, as they must have realised that the ark had rested in the mountains.

The recession of the waters would have many significant effects. In the middle of continents, large lakes would be left. Some of these would burst their banks, gouging out large canyons. Indeed, the formation of the Grand Canyon can be described in this way.

Morris also records a remarkable discussion on the dates involved in the end of the Flood.

In OT times, a distinction was made between civil and religious calendars. At the first Passover, the seventh month of the civil year became the first month of the religious year. Passover itself was set at the fourteenth day of this month. Thus Jesus rose from the dead on the seventeenth day of the seventh month, according to the civil calendar. Remarkably, this is the same day as the ark rested on the mountains of Ararat, and there was indeed to be a resurrection of a dead world.

---

[1] Morris, H.M., *The Genesis Record*, (Baker: 1976) p206

18.3 Noah's Experiments

So it came to pass, at the end of forty days, that Noah opened the window of the ark which he had made. Then he sent out a raven, which kept going to and fro until the waters had dried up from the earth. He also sent out from himself a dove, to see if the waters had receded from the face of the ground. But the dove found no resting place for the sole of her foot, and she returned into the ark to him, for the waters were on the face of the whole earth. So he put out his hand and took her, and drew her into the ark to himself. And he waited yet another seven days, and again he sent the dove out from the ark. Then the dove came to him in the evening, and behold, a freshly plucked olive leaf was in her mouth; and Noah knew that the waters had receded from the earth. So he waited yet another seven days and sent out the dove, which did not return again to him anymore.

Noah performed a remarkable series of experiments, to see whether the land was safe enough for them to disembark. That this exercise was necessary, demonstrates the devastation of the world. It also demonstrates that God does not always tell us everything. Matthew Henry observes: "Though God had told Noah particularly when the flood would come, even to a day (Gen 7:4), yet he did not give him a particular account by revelation at what times, and by what steps, it should go away".[2]

A friend of mine told me this anecdote. There came a time in his career, where he thought he ought to change jobs. A new opportunity with another company opened up. He prayed over the job and felt that God was showing him clearly that it was right to go for the new job, which he got. Some years later, a similar situation arose. He prayed and prayed, but got no definitive answer, until he asked God why He wasn't giving him an answer. My friend then felt very strongly that God was saying that this time he needed to use the brain that God had given him, to work it out for himself.

The raven, being a scavenger, found no difficulty in staying out of the ark. However the dove needed somewhere to land. The initial return of the dove suggests that there was insufficient land for it at first. On the second occasion he sent out the dove, it returned with an olive leaf. So

---

[2] Revised Matthew Henry Commentary.

seedlings must have been able to sprout quickly, or else had somehow, miraculously survived.

On its third flight, the dove goes away for ever. Doves cannot hover and scavenge, so this was a clear sign to Noah that there was food and perch for the dove.

Where did the dove get its olive leaf from? It is unlikely that a seedling could have sprouted so quickly, so it may have been part of a matting of vegetation. That would explain why the existence of an olive leaf does not make Noah open the door and disembark. When the dove fails to return, however, there is a clear signal that there is suitable land.

18.4 Disembarking

And it came to pass in the six hundred and first year, in the first month, the first day of the month that the waters were dried up from the earth; and Noah removed the covering of the ark and looked, and indeed the surface of the ground was dry. And in the second month, on the twenty-seventh day of the month, the earth was dried. Then God spoke to Noah, saying, "Go out of the ark, you and your wife, and your sons and your sons' wives with you. Bring out with you every living thing of all flesh that is with you: birds and cattle and every creeping thing that creeps on the earth, so that they may abound on the earth, and be fruitful and multiply on the earth." So Noah went out, and his sons and his wife and his sons' wives with him. Every animal, every creeping thing, every bird, and whatever creeps on the earth, according to their families, went out of the ark.

God had promised Noah that he would survive the Flood. Now was the moment for God to keep His promise. God instructs Noah to release all the animals that he had been carrying on the Ark. Once again, the various kinds of animals are emphasised.

The world that Noah and his family entered was very different from that of half a year ago. Peter reminds us, "the world that then existed perished, being flooded with water." (2 Peter 3:6). It is likely that the world was desolate. There could have been a silence around the place. Prior to the Flood, the world was full of people and animals. After the Flood, all the people and nephesh land animals existed within a few yards of the Ark.

The new world was very different from the old world. In the old world, there was far more land than sea. In this new world, there is far more sea than land. I suspect that immediately after the Flood, the land would still be joined together. But huge geological effects would soon divide the land into modern continents.

Before the Flood, there was no rain. After the Flood, the clouds could gather without warning, and rain would fall. No doubt this would have terrified the eight people, but God graciously saw to that problem, as we will see in the next chapter.

Before the Flood, there were hills and valleys. Now there are mountains, capped with snow, and deep rift valleys.

Most scientists, including creationists, accept that there was an Ice Age at some point in the past. With their usual over-exaggeration of time scales, evolutionists suppose that the Ice Age was many millions of years ago, and that it lasted a couple of million years. Creationists would argue that the dating methods used to suggest these ages are not valid. There is no reason to suppose that the Ice Age lasted longer than a few hundred – maybe a thousand – years. Some early creationists supposed that the Ice Age covered the entire Earth. This is not the case. We accept that ice covered about a third of the surface. In other words, there were polar caps like today, but more extensive.

We have already noted the tremendous geological effects that a worldwide Flood would cause. For the first time, the atmosphere would contain dust, around which raindrops could coalesce. The atmospheric dust would almost certainly be much greater than today. There was, after all, an increase in dust over most of the world after the Krakatoa eruption. Also, we should note that the climatic engines would be entirely different after the Flood to what they were before. The Earth was an even all-over regular temperature before the Flood, verified by the number of coal seams in all parts of the world. The harmonising effect of the pre-diluvian hydrological cycle – the "fountains of the deep" – would no longer be in operation. Instead, we have the current hydrological cycle of evaporation and precipitation.

Some models suggest that the early days of the introduction of this new hydrological cycle would transfer large amounts of water to suddenly colder regions, therefore falling as snow. Many scientists have written articles for creationist peer-reviewed scientific journals, such as Creation Research Society Quarterly (CRSQ) and Creation Ex Nihilo

Technical Journal (CEN TJ), giving mechanisms for how the Ice Age could have been triggered by the end of the Flood. Suffice it for this book simply to say that it would seem inevitable that the end of the Flood would have major climatic effects, probably including an Ice Age. The very fact of the Ice Age indicates some worldwide catastrophe. Henry Morris says "Evolutionary glacial geologists have been debating for nearly a hundred years as to what may have caused such an Ice Age, without coming to any consensus. The rocks which supposedly correspond to earlier ages practically all give evidence of a worldwide subtropical climate, and the cause of this condition is also a mystery."[3]

Another major effect of the Flood is in covering vast areas of the Earth's crust in sedimentary rock. This also is the subject of much scientific work published in CRSQ and CEN TJ. Hardly an issue of these journals goes by, without a major analysis of some part of the world, analysing how its sedimentation may have come into being. Creationists differ on how much of the world's sedimentary rock was produced by the Flood, some arguing that it all was, some arguing that as much as 80% of sedimentation may have occurred after the Flood. I am more convinced that the greater part of the world's sedimentation was caused by the Flood. This is more for Biblical reasons than anything else, as I remain convinced of the completeness of the Semitic line of descent, as detailed in Genesis 10.

Whatever the arguments as to the exact creationist methodology of sedimentation, creationists are agreed that sedimentation can happen quickly. There are many evidences in the literature of rapid fossilisation, which requires rapid sedimentation.

Think of the evidence of fossils themselves. Dead bodies just do not hang around for long. Evolutionists require that large dinosaur fossils, for example, took thousands of years to become entombed. Imagine a half-fossilised dinosaur. Half its dead body is already fossilised and the other half of the skeleton is sticking out into the air. This just would not happen. We know that bones rot as does flesh, though not quite as quickly. For a complete skeleton to be fossilised, it would seem that the surrounding sedimentation would have to occur very swiftly. Such a scenario is, in my mind, best explained by the swirling sediments of the Flood. As Ken Ham has frequently observed; what would we expect to

---

[3] Morris, H.M., *The Bible Has the Answer*, (Master Books: 1987)

find if there really had been a Flood – "Billions of dead things covered in rock layers laid down in water all over the Earth."[4] And that is, of course, precisely what we do find.

18.5 Noah at Worship

Then Noah built an altar to the LORD, and took of every clean animal and of every clean bird, and offered burnt offerings on the altar. And the LORD smelled a soothing aroma. Then the LORD said in His heart, "I will never again curse the ground for man's sake, although the imagination of man's heart is evil from his youth; nor will I again destroy every living thing as I have done. While the earth remains, Seedtime and harvest, Cold and heat, Winter and summer, And day and night Shall not cease."

We observed earlier that Noah took more clean animals into the ark. Some translators suggest he took seven of every clean kind – some suggest seven pairs. Woodmorappe[5] plays safe in his analysis, by assuming a "worst case" scenario of seven pairs. This would still not involve many animals. If we assume that the definition of a clean animal in Noah's time was the same as that later in Moses's time, then the numbers would be small. For example, cattle, sheep and goats are all closely related, and are probably members of the same baramin. So Moses would not need seven goats, seven sheep and seven cows – he would only need seven ruminants.

It is these clean animals which are the most usual creatures for sacrifice. So Noah takes clean animals and birds and sheds their blood on the altar, because "without shedding of blood there is no remission". (Hebrews 9:22) Moreover, Noah burns the carcasses, which symbolises a complete dedication of the offering to God. This is the sort of sacrifice referred to in Romans 12:1. "I beseech you therefore, brethren, by the mercies of God, that you present your bodies a living sacrifice, holy, acceptable to God, which is your reasonable service." In the immediate aftermath of the Flood, Noah, a man who God treats as righteous, because he found grace in the eyes of God, begins his life in the new

---

[4] This seems to be one of Ken Ham's favourite sayings, and well worth remembering!

[5] Woodmorappe, J., *Noah's Ark: A Feasibility Study*, (ICR:1996)

world, by worshipping God and completely dedicating his life to Him. This is a pattern for us. I am pleased that Genesis contains such touches as these. These are not the myths and legends of a bygone age. These are the living monuments to a life lived by grace. Because it is only by grace that we are saved, Noah becomes a pattern to us by his obedience, worship and actions.

Then God gives a remarkable promise to Noah – the so-called Noachan Covenant. He promises that He will not again send a Flood. This is all the more remarkable, because God tells Noah that He is not starry-eyed about the nature of Noah's descendents: "the imagination of man's heart is evil from his youth". Nevertheless, the LORD promises, using His own divine Name, that He will not destroy all living things (*nephesh*) again in a Flood. The consequences of this remarkable covenant we will examine in the next chapter.

19. The Covenant of Common Grace

Read Genesis 9

The importance of Genesis 9 cannot, in my mind, be understated. Yet it is a passage of scripture much neglected. It is, perhaps, less exciting to the creation scientists than the preceding three chapters, as it does not imply the same quantity of scientific research. The new breed of creation historians is likely to be attracted to the genealogies of Genesis 10. But this leaves what I believe to be a fascinating chapter. Theologically, Genesis 9 is explosive.

In this chapter, we learn about God's covenant with the whole of humankind. We also learn that the single family now living in the world is not perfect, and cannot even now fully obey God's commands.

19.1. The Position of the Noahic Covenant in Scripture

We have already learned that Noah was a man under grace, not under law. Therefore, God's covenant with Noah, and hence with all humankind, is a covenant of grace. It is not superseded by the Abrahamic Covenant. This added a specific promise to the faithful and to God's people. Nor was it superseded by the Mosaic Covenant, which symbolised and typified the seriousness of sin, by the requirements of the law and the sacrifices.

God's covenant with Noah is therefore rightly called the covenant of common grace. The graciousness of God is revealed to the whole of humanity. God makes specific promises to the whole of humanity. He lays down patterns of righteous government, which transcend all boundaries of nationality or religion. We can even go on to say that the Noahic Covenant is not superseded by the New Covenant in the Blood of

Jesus Christ – rather this is a fulfilment of God's plans and purposes from the time of the Garden, and certainly seen through the beginning of this new post-Flood world.

19.2. Blessings and Food

So God blessed Noah and his sons, and said to them: "Be fruitful and multiply, and fill the earth. And the fear of you and the dread of you shall be on every beast of the earth, on every bird of the air, on all that move on the earth, and on all the fish of the sea. They are given into your hand. Every moving thing that lives shall be food for you. I have given you all things, even as the green herbs. But you shall not eat flesh with its life, that is, its blood."

The first thing we read is that this new First Family are blessed by God. We read later in Genesis that blessing does not imply the sinlessness of the one who is blessed. Nevertheless, God gives Noah's family the best possible start to the new world.

God then renews the cultural mandate of Genesis 1:28. There is, however, a subtle difference. In Genesis 1:28, God told mankind to subdue the earth and fill it. Mankind was to have dominion over all the animals. In Genesis 9:2, however, God makes it clear that there is a new relationship between man and animal. It is a relationship of fear. Even among the most ferocious of animals, there is a wariness of people. Many mighty hunting animals instinctively know that people are their worst enemies. But this was not how it was meant to be in a sinless world. In the beginning, lions were meant to lie down with lambs, and all were to eat only plants. Now in this sin-affected world, there are carnivorous animals. Man's position would be dangerous, were the animals not to have some fear of man. But this also symbolises the end of innocence about the relationship between man and animals. If animals were to have a fear of people, then they were right to do so. Throughout today's world, the human race is frequently the greatest enemy any species of animal can have. It is not just the dodo that is extinct as a direct result of people's actions.

The other change in our relationship with animals is that God now allows humans to eat other animals. We are given sanction to become carnivorous – or at least omnivorous. I have a respect for vegetarians, though I cannot myself be a vegetarian. Our diet needs the sort of proteins we can only get directly from meat, poultry and fish. It is true that there are substitutes – and many readers of this book may well be vegetarians. I have met vegetarians who are that way inclined, because they just don't like meat. That seems fair enough to me. I am concerned, however, that the vegetarianism of some Christians may be influenced by a sort of latent evolutionism – viewing animals sentimentally as closer to humans in the evolutionary chain. It seems to me that God is acknowledging that, in a sinful fallen world, there is a requirement for our post-diluvian imperfect bodies, with imperfect digestive systems, to ingest protein in a faster, more palatable form than before.

God is not here giving complete freedom to eat what we want. He restricts the right to eat blood. This would seem to be in order to emphasise again the significance of *nephesh* life forms over the non-nephesh. Once again, we are being reminded of the importance of blood, as it is only through blood that sins can be forgiven.

19.3. For Lifeblood a Reckoning

"Surely for your lifeblood I will demand a reckoning; from the hand of every beast I will require it, and from the hand of man. From the hand of every man's brother I will require the life of man. Whoever sheds man's blood, By man his blood shall be shed; For in the image of God He made man."

These two verses are among the most controversial in the whole of Genesis, and some readers might not like my analysis. There are many creationists who would disagree with my opinion on these points.

It would seem to me that these verses justify the destruction of an animal that has killed a man. Few would argue with that point. Any establishment that keeps animals tends to view with alarm any occasion when an animal overcomes its "natural" fear of man and kills someone.

It also appears to me, however, that verse 6 sanctions the death penalty for murder. I would argue that this verse illustrates that capital punishment is the acceptable and just punishment for any person who deliberately takes another persons life.

I have differentiated above, between the Mosaic Covenant and the Noahic Covenant. The Mosaic Covenant is most certainly superseded by the New Covenant of Jesus. For this reason, the many death penalties described in the Law for various sins are not to be translated into the law of current Gentile state governments. That these laws illustrate the seriousness of sins is undeniable. That the Mosaic laws define the various activities, which are to be labelled as sins, is also the case. But the Mosaic death penalties are equivalent to a loss of salvation rather than a blueprint for a 21st Century penal system. Thus, were there to be a call for a re-introduction of the death penalty for homosexuality, adultery, or children disrespecting their parents, I would find no Biblical support.

Yet one death penalty is exceptional. It is the death penalty for murder. The fact that this death penalty alone is introduced under the Noahic Covenant of common grace, rather than the Mosaic Covenant for the Israelites, suggests that the death penalty is as much part of the current natural order of things, as the post-diluvian animals' fear of human beings.

Many readers, who have travelled with me through this book, will feel unable to join me in these views. I respect that, but ask that you respect that, for many Christians, our support for the death penalty for murder, which seems so incongruous to many, is based on Genesis 9:6, and not on some misapplication of the Levitical Laws.

"And as for you, be fruitful and multiply; Bring forth abundantly in the earth And multiply in it."

In this verse, God reinstates His command that people are to fill the world. It is this command which we see is resisted by Nimrod and others, and leads directly to the rebellion at Babel, in Genesis 11.

19.4. The Statement of the Covenant

Then God spoke to Noah and to his sons with him, saying: "And as for Me, behold, I establish My covenant with you and with your descendants after you, and with every living creature that is with you: the birds, the cattle, and every beast of the earth with you, of all that go out of the ark, every beast of the earth. Thus I establish My covenant with you: Never again shall all flesh be cut off by the waters of the flood; never again shall there be a flood to destroy the earth."

Covenants in the Bible, like covenants today, are legal documents. It is remarkable that God chooses to bind Himself to a legal document. It is even more remarkable, when you realise that it is impossible for us to keep our side of the agreement. Not only that, but God knows we cannot keep our side of the agreement, and delivers a one-sided covenant.

Who does God establish this covenant with? The subjects of the covenant include everybody – Noah, his family and all his descendants, as well as all the nephesh creatures of the world. This indicates that it is a covenant of blood, even though blood is not specifically mentioned. Nevertheless, the connection between all the creatures mentioned is the lifeblood.

What does God require from us? Remarkably, the actual legal part of the covenant does not require anything on our part. The rules given in the first few verses of chapter 9 point us to the seriousness of sin, but they do not, in and of themselves, constitute part of the covenant.

What does God bind Himself to? God is infinite, all powerful and all knowing. That God should choose to limit Himself in any way is mind-boggling enough. But in this statement of the covenant, He promises never again to cut off all flesh by a Flood. He promises not to destroy the world again by water.

The test of any covenant is this: have the parties kept to the terms of the agreement. In the Noahic Covenant, God placed no demands upon us, so we have nothing to keep. As far as God's part is concerned, we can observe that He has kept His side of the bargain.

We ought not to put God to the test. Yet when He allows us to test Him, we find Him to be completely faithful, completely trustworthy. That is the nature of the God, in whom we believe.

19.5. The Covenant Sealed

Every covenant needs signatures or seals to make it legal. Both parties must sign, to confirm that they agree to do what they have covenanted to do. In a one-sided covenant, only one signature is necessary. And what a glorious signature God gives us!

> And God said: "This is the sign of the covenant which I make between Me and you, and every living creature that is with you, for perpetual generations: "I set My rainbow in the cloud, and it shall be for the sign of the covenant between Me and the earth. It shall be, when I bring a cloud over the earth, that the rainbow shall be seen in the cloud; and I will remember My covenant which is between Me and you and every living creature of all flesh; the waters shall never again become a flood to destroy all flesh. The rainbow shall be in the cloud, and I will look on it to remember the everlasting covenant between God and every living creature of all flesh that is on the earth." And God said to Noah, "This is the sign of the covenant which I have established between Me and all flesh that is on the earth."

Some creationists are unhappy with a dogmatic statement that there was no rain before the Flood. Yet if there was no rain before the Flood, there would have been no rainbows before the Flood. It seems to make sense that this event is the first appearance of either clouds or rainbows.

If we believe that rainbows happened before the Flood, or if you believe there never was a Flood, then this passage takes on the form of a "Just So" story – a neat little legend, all designed to explain why we see a coloured band in the sky. If we accept that this is the very first rainbow, how would Noah and his family have felt when they saw it?

When we see rainbows today, they have the same meaning. They are caused by the diffraction of light through droplets of water in the atmosphere. They usually happen when the sun shines during the rain. They are a reminder that, however hard the rain may be, we can be assured that there is insufficient water in today's atmosphere to cause another Flood.

There have been plenty of local floods throughout history. If Noah's Flood was just another local flood, then what is so good about God's covenantal promise? If there had been plenty of rainbows before, then what is the value of God's signature?

It is my contention that these wonderful natural occurrences are there to bolster our faith, and remind us that God always keeps His promises and is always to be trusted.

19.6. Sin, Shame and Curses

Now the sons of Noah who went out of the ark were Shem, Ham, and Japheth. And Ham was the father of Canaan. These three were the sons of Noah, and from these the whole earth was populated. And Noah began to be a farmer, and he planted a vineyard. Then he drank of the wine and was drunk, and became uncovered in his tent. And Ham, the father of Canaan, saw the nakedness of his father, and told his two brothers outside. But Shem and Japheth took a garment, laid it on both their shoulders, and went backward and covered the nakedness of their father. Their faces were turned away, and they did not see their father's nakedness.

When we read the genealogy of Adam, we read that he had other sons and daughters. In the case of Noah, however, we read that he had just these three sons. The context suggests that he had only these sons. It is therefore from these three sons and their wives that the whole human race is descended.

The passage also reminds us that Ham was the father of Canaan. More on this later.

We are told that Noah began farming. This was entirely in keeping with God's order in creation. In Genesis 2, we read that Adam was to work the Garden. Noah, likewise, is not intended to sit back and do nothing. As Paul puts it in 2 Thes. 3:10 "For even when we were with you, we commanded you this: If anyone will not work, neither shall he eat". It was never intended for humanity to have a life of leisure. Mankind was made to work.

The sort of husbandry described before the Flood seems to be concerned with grain. Now Noah plants a vineyard. Wine is not produced from a vineyard easily, so we must assume that these short sentences are actually summarising a fairly extensive period of time. This gives plenty of time for his sons to have had their own sons.

We then have this strange account of Noah getting drunk. Matthew Poole says this:

Either through ignorance and inexperience of the nature and strength of that liquor, or through the infirmity of the flesh, which was tempted by its great and, to him, new pleasantness, and by the refreshment he found in it under the weary labours of his body, and the sad thoughts of his mind, for the desolate condition of the world.[1]

We are not told the reason for this problem of Noah's. We can assume that it indicates that he drank too much. Becoming drunk can leave us in all sorts of humiliating positions. At this time, the wearing of clothes would still be strongly symbolic of our guilt before God, and our need to hide our shame. The fact that Noah is uncovered suggests that he has temporarily lost that shame.

There is, however, no indication that this is a major problem. There would probably have been no problem at all, had Ham behaved as a loving son. Ham was himself a father at this point. Indeed, since Canaan was his youngest son, he clearly had experience as a father. So his example of son-ship is a poor example to his sons. What Ham should have done is to cover his father and say no more about it, except perhaps to his father. Instead, he compounds the shame, by wanting his brothers to join in his amusement at his father's condition. Fortunately, his brothers were more circumspect. They probably also had sons at this point, so wanted to set an example of respect, by covering Noah, walking backwards, without looking at him.

19.7. Cursed be Canaan

This brings us to the subject of the curse that Noah utters and its meaning. Much nonsense has been spoken over this curse. Let us start by examining what this curse is not.

The curse has sometimes been described as the curse of Ham. Following this, certain interpreters, always white, have suggested that the curse involved Ham becoming black.

It is unlikely that Ham was black. It is most likely that all three sons were middle-brown. Blackness of skin is caused by a pigment called melanin. All humans have this pigment. Some have the capability to produce more than others. White people have little capability of producing this pigment. Black people have more. We will discuss the dispersal of races and nations more in the next chapter. For the moment,

---

[1] Poole, M., *Commentary of the Bible,*

we will settle by saying that the idea that the curse of Ham caused blackness of skin is an abominable idea, thought up only by white supremacists who want a "biblical" excuse for racism. In fact, such a view has no merit, and has no biblical warrant.

Blackness and whiteness of skin is more likely to have developed later, after the Babel incident, as people were scattered throughout the world. Neither whiteness nor blackness confers any special merit or demerit on the person. All such characteristics must have been part of the original genetic make-up of humanity.[2]

In fact, it should be noted that the curse was not pronounced on Ham but on Canaan.

> So Noah awoke from his wine, and knew what his younger son had done to him. Then he said: "Cursed be Canaan; A servant of servants He shall be to his brethren." And he said: "Blessed be the LORD, The God of Shem, And may Canaan be his servant. May God enlarge Japheth, And may he dwell in the tents of Shem; And may Canaan be his servant."

Ham's actions, though reprehensible and disrespectful, did not constitute a major "cursable" offence. We have to assume that Noah was aware, prophetically or otherwise, of greater offences either already caused or soon to be caused by Canaan. That Canaan is specifically cursed also gives the lie to the theory that the curse caused blackness – Canaanites were not black.

Canaanites later in the Bible were the usurpers of the land that God had promised to Abraham. The Israelites were told to completely destroy these Canaanites, because their worship of false gods was particularly offensive to God. The failure of the Israelites completely to destroy the Canaanites was a major source of problems throughout Israel's history. Nevertheless, we can see proof that the curse applies only because of evil among individuals, not to a whole race. For example, Rahab of Jericho was a Canaanite, yet she ended up not only being spared when the Israelites attacked Jericho[3], but is listed as an ancestor of Jesus[4].

---

[2] For a more detailed discussion of why those who take the Bible, and Genesis in particular, seriously should not be racist, please see One Blood, by Ken Ham, published by Master Books.

[3] Josh 6:17

[4] Matt 1:5

And Noah lived after the flood three hundred and fifty years. So all the days of Noah were nine hundred and fifty years; and he died.

Noah lived for a long time after the Flood. He would have been contemporaneous with many other Biblical figures, including Abraham. There was obviously a lot more for Noah to do and say. Mike Gascoigne has documented some fascinating legends concerning Noah's teaching ministry after the Flood.[5] But the Bible just finishes by telling us that Noah lived another 350 years, and was 950 when he died. The Flood was the one, great important episode in Noah's life, teaching us the importance of grace, faith and obedience. The writer of Genesis doesn't think there are any more spiritual lessons to draw from Noah's life, so he exits stage left.

---

[5] Gascoigne, M, *Forgotten History of the Western People*, Anno Mundi: 2002

20. The Table of Nations

Read Genesis 10

Now this is the genealogy of the sons of Noah: Shem, Ham, and Japheth. And sons were born to them after the flood.

Genesis 10 can be taken as a historical record, almost separately from the rest of Genesis. As a historical document, it is of great import, yet it is a history rarely taught in secular, state schools. The chapter has given rise to a fascinating new area of study for the creationist – Creation History. This history dares to answer the question: "Where did we actually all come from?" In giving the answer "from Noah and his Ark", we are led into new areas of research. This chapter can only scratch the surface of such studies, and for further information, the reader is referred to the books "After the Flood" by Bill Cooper and "Forgotten History of the Western People" by Mike Gascoigne.[1,2]

The accuracy of the Table of Nations has come under attack over the last century, as has the rest of Genesis. Recently, however, its accuracy has come under attack by Bible-believing creationists, who believe everything else concerning Genesis, including a six day creation. These critical creationists are mostly geologists (though not all creationist geologists would subscribe to their views). They follow a theory known as Recolonisation Theory. This suggests that the bulk of the Earth's sedimentation occurred **after** the Flood, rather than during it. As evidence, they point to the geological column, and explain this by effects as creatures recolonise parts of the Earth following the Flood.

It will not have escaped your notice that this author is sceptical about the claims of recolonisation theory. To be fair, the reader will want to examine their articles. A good starting point is probably the recolonisation website.[3] Paul Garner has also written a detailed

---

[1] Cooper, W, *After the Flood*, New Wine Press: 1995
[2] Gascoigne, M, *Forgotten History of the Western People*, Anno Mundi: 2002
[3] http://www.recolonisation.org.uk/

justification of recolonisation theory.[4] For example, Garner illustrates a problem with conventional Flood geology thus:

> Some creationists, such as Whitcomb and Morris (1961, p270-288), have tried to explain the fossil successions as a record of the order of burial of creatures during the Flood. In this view, the fossil successions represent: (i) the progressive burial of pre-Flood habitats as the waters rose, (ii) the different abilities of creatures to escape burial, and (iii) the effects of water sorting. However, problems with this theory have been expressed by evolutionists and creationists alike. Very few specific studies of fossil zonation have been carried out to test this idea. When examined in detail, the logical predictions of the model fail to correspond to the order of the fossils found in the rocks. To give one example: why is it that sloths - extremely slow-moving mammals that should have been overwhelmed quite early in the Flood - do not appear in the fossil record until the Upper Eocene? Moreover, the ecological zonation model assumes that virtually the entire geological record was formed during the Flood, neglecting the possibility that some of the sediments were laid down during the unstable centuries following the catastrophe. [5]

The views of the recolonisation party have been equally strenuously refuted by McIntosh, Taylor and Edmondson. In this extract, they criticise one of the recolonisation theorists interpretation of the Hebrew word '*machah*'.

> Although Robinson's exegesis of 'machah' may not be the key reason for espousing their Flood model, they have to face the biblical implications of their position. One can rightly ask, 'So what happened to all the air-breathing, land creatures buried in the Flood?' This has led to the proposal by Robinson13 and supported by the rest of the group,14 that 'machah' (translated 'destroy' in Genesis 6:7 and other places) means 'blot out without trace'.

> Their admission that the biblical exegesis is not the key reason for espousing their Flood model, shows the weakness of their thinking. Their science is driving their interpretation of Scripture, and not the other way

---

[4] Garner, P., *The Age of the Earth: Geology and the Deluge*, http://www.amen.org.uk/eh/science/flodpg/flodpg3.htm 2000
[5] *ibid*

round. From this unproven (and in our opinion false) premise, they construct a model that owes more to a desired allegiance to the geological column than to Scripture. In fact their model runs into conflict with post-Flood Scriptural chronology and timescales.

We admit that it is not always easy to interpret science from a 'Bible-first' mentality. There are puzzles to solve, but these are far less perplexing than the massive post-Flood inundations required by their model. Such a model raises great questions about whether God meant what He said when He stated 'neither shall there any more be a flood to destroy the earth' (Genesis 9:11). [6]

In the view of this author, this goes to the heart of the problem. If we are to accept the word of the recolonisation theorists, then there have to be gaps in the genealogies of Genesis 10, in order to allow for the extra years required. Most of the recolonisation theorists add about 4000 years to the age of the Earth, though Robinson goes further, making the age of the Earth about 21000 years.[7] Whatever the value of the geological observations and suppositions, such an interpretation of Genesis 10 strikes this author as *eisegesis* rather than *exegesis*. Exegesis looks at scripture and works out what it means. Eisegesis reads into scripture our presuppositions. Eisegesis is a hard accusation to make of any scholar, but I cannot find the gaps in the genealogies of Genesis 10 naturally, unless I first suppose that I need a longer timescale than 6000 years for the age of the Earth. It is for this reason that this work will assume no gaps in, at least, the primary Shemite genealogy.

In the remainder of this chapter, we will conjecture on where these tribes listed in Genesis 10 may have gone. It is our supposition that all the nations of the world are descended from these.

The research that follows is taken from the wrings of Morris[8], and, more particularly, Cooper[9].

---

[6] McIntosh, A., Taylor, S., Edmondson, T., McIntosh, Taylor and Edmondson reply to Flood Models, CEN Technical Journal **14**(3):80–82 December 2000

[7] Robinson, S.J., *Interpreting the Fossil Record*, 2004 http://www.noahsarkzoofarm.co.uk/research/interpretations.shtml

[8] Morris, H., *The Genesis Record*, Evangelical Press: 1976

[9] Cooper, W, *After the Flood*, New Wine Press: 1995

20.1. Japhethites

The sons of Japheth were Gomer, Magog, Madai, Javan, Tubal, Meshech, and Tiras. The sons of Gomer were Ashkenaz, Riphath, and Togarmah. The sons of Javan were Elishah, Tarshish, Kittim, and Dodanim. From these the coastland peoples of the Gentiles were separated into their lands, everyone according to his language, according to their families, into their nations.

Japheth seems to be identified with a number of legendary figures; Jupiter, of Roman mythology, Iapetus of Greek legend, and Iyapeti among the Aryans of India. It would appear then that the majority of Japhethites migrated West into Europe, though some went East into Persia and India.

Gomer appears to be associated with an area known as Cimmeria, north of the Black Sea – preserved in the name Crimea. His name may also be preserved in the names Germany and Cymru (Wales). Of Gomer's sons, Ashkenaz is associated with Germany. To this day, Germanic Jews are known as Ashkenazi. This name is preserved in Scandia – Scandinavia, and Saxon. Riphath is the father of Paphlagonians and Carpathians. Togarmah seems to be the ancestor of the Armenians.

Magog is the ancestor of peoples around Georgia, though the capital of Georgia, Tblisi, commemorates Tubal. Madai is associated with the Medes, though these also merge with a Hamitic group. Javan refers to Ionia, in Greece, as does Elishah, from which we get Hellenic, referring to Greece. Tarshish seems to be Spain, while Kittim is Cyprus. Meshech is preserved in the word Moscow, so would appear to be the ancestor of the Russian peoples.

It is these Japhethitic peoples who are most commonly referred to as Gentiles (v5). We are reminded that their division is due to their languages. These peoples may have started to migrate early, because many (though not all) of their languages are from a common language group – the Indo-European group.

20.2. Hamites

More space is given to Hamitic people, and they seem to have covered more of the globe between them.

The sons of Ham were Cush, Mizraim, Put, and Canaan.

The sons of Cush were Seba, Havilah, Sabtah, Raamah, and Sabtechah; and the sons of Raamah were Sheba and Dedan. Cush begot Nimrod; he began to be a mighty one on the earth. He was a mighty hunter before the LORD; therefore it is said, "Like Nimrod the mighty hunter before the LORD." And the beginning of his kingdom was Babel, Erech, Accad, and Calneh, in the land of Shinar. From that land he went to Assyria and built Nineveh, Rehoboth Ir, Calah, and Resen between Nineveh and Calah (that is the principal city).

Mizraim begot Ludim, Anamim, Lehabim, Naphtuhim, Pathrusim, and Casluhim (from whom came the Philistines and Caphtorim).

Canaan begot Sidon his firstborn, and Heth; the Jebusite, the Amorite, and the Girgashite; the Hivite, the Arkite, and the Sinite; the Arvadite, the Zemarite, and the Hamathite. Afterward the families of the Canaanites were dispersed. And the border of the Canaanites was from Sidon as you go toward Gerar, as far as Gaza; then as you go toward Sodom, Gomorrah, Admah, and Zeboiim, as far as Lasha.

These were the sons of Ham, according to their families, according to their languages, in their lands and in their nations.

Cush is a word used throughout the Bible and elsewhere for Ethiopia. The sons of Cush would therefore appear to constitute most of the ancestors of the black Africans. It would appear that they migrated first through the Arabian peninsula, then across into Ethiopia.

Of Cush's sons, Seba is one of many candidates as the original Sheba.

Cush's most famous son was Nimrod. The genealogies break off, to give something of a story about Nimrod. We will briefly analyse this, though some more detail will be retained for Genesis 11. Nimrod, we are told, became "a mighty one on the Earth". This would suggest a warrior. The fact that so many cities of his are listed, suggests that he was a military leader, setting up a military dictatorship. The phrase "mighty hunter before the LORD" is better translated as "mighty hunter *in the face of* the LORD." His actions were those of rebellion against God. As one of his main cities was Babylon, it seems appropriate to link him with the Tower of Babel incident. It should be noted that some of his cities were in Assyria. This implies that he invaded that territory.

Mizraim is Egypt and Put is Libya.

Cannan, the one who was cursed, has some interesting sons. Sidon would appear to be Phoenicia. Heth gives rise to the Hittites. In cuneiform script, this sometimes reads *Khittae*. It is suggested that, following the collapse of the Hittite Empire, Hittites moved East to Cathay (Khittae) becoming the Chines people. Similarly, the Sinites probably moved East. To this day, we refer to things appertaining to China using a sino-prefix (Sino-American relations, Sino-Japanese war etc). These people seem to be mentioned in Isaiah 49:12. Thus, the Hittites and Sinites could be the progenitors of East Asian mongoloid peoples. When the Bering "Bridge" is taken into account, they are probably also the ancestors of Native American peoples.

As with the Japhethites, we read that the languages caused the division (v20).

20.3. Shemites (Semites)

And children were born also to Shem, the father of all the children of Eber, the brother of Japheth the elder. The sons of Shem were Elam, Asshur, Arphaxad, Lud, and Aram.

The sons of Aram were Uz, Hul, Gether, and Mash.

Arphaxad begot Salah, and Salah begot Eber. To Eber were born two sons: the name of one was Peleg, for in his days the earth was divided; and his brother's name was Joktan. Joktan begot Almodad, Sheleph, Hazarmaveth, Jerah, Hadoram, Uzal, Diklah, Obal, Abimael, Sheba, Ophir, Havilah, and Jobab. All these were the sons of Joktan. And their dwelling place was from Mesha as you go toward Sephar, the mountain of the east.

These were the sons of Shem, according to their families, according to their languages, in their lands, according to their nations.

The writer firstly wants to emphasise that Shem is the ancestor of all the children of Eber – the Hebrews. Then we get into detail.

Lud was Lydia and Aram was Aramean people, from where we get Aramaic. The Elamites are mentioned in conjunction with their king, Chedorlaomer, mentioned in Genesis 14.

Asshur is the progenitor of the Assyrians, though Nimrod invaded their territory, so that Assyrian people were partly Semitic and partly Hamitic.

Arphaxad is part of the blood-line, eventually leading to Jesus. So is his son Salah, and so is Salah's son Eber. Eber is of the same generation as Nimrod. Thus, Eber probably lived through the Tower of Babel crisis. This crisis lives on in the name of one of Eber's sons, Peleg, which means division, "for in his days the earth was divided". This is probably a reference to the division of the peoples of the world, by their linguistic confusion.

Genesis 10 is a fascinating chapter. It is easy to skip over it, thinking it dry. I would urge the reader to further research in the books, mentioned earlier, by Cooper and by Gascoigne.

After all this genealogical detail, Noah signs off.

These were the families of the sons of Noah, according to their generations, in their nations; and from these the nations were divided on the earth after the   flood.

21. The Tower of Babel

It is important not to underestimate the Tower of Babel incident. This incident is not just a local myth affecting a small group of people. The incident affected the entire population of the world, and, as such, was just as global in its extent as the Flood. It is the lot of liberal theologians to pick holes in the veracity of scriptures such as these. However, there is no doubt in the mind of this author that the incident is historically true, and explains a great deal of subsequent history.

The evolution of language puzzles scholars. How did it develop among the so-called cavemen? Several theories have been developed by evolutionists, the most popular of which have cavemen inventing word for common objects, trying to contact each other, or making noises during collective efforts of work. These three theories are sometimes referred to as the mamma theory, the hey-you theory and the yo-he-ho theory (I kid you not). To be fair, several more intelligent theories have been developed recently, but they all suffer from the same problem as biological Darwinism. Theories on the evolution of language postulate the development of complex forms from simple ones, yet the observations of real languages show simple, or at least chaotic, languages developing from complex. For example, German has a well-developed grammar, featuring three genders and four cases. Latin has an even more complex and well-ordered grammar. Yet English, which has developed from these and others, uses no gender and no cases, in so far as word mutation is concerned. If the evolution of languages were true, we would expect Latin to have developed from English, rather than the other way around.

Even more problematic is the fact that languages did not all develop from one root language. There are groups of languages. Languages within the groups seem to be related. Thus we can see relationships within the Indo-European group – e.g. Father is pére in French, pater in Latin, pîtr in Sanskrit. Yet none of these languages bears any relationship to Korean. More confusingly, none of the Indo-European languages seems to bear any relationship to Basque.

These problems become solvable, as soon as we assume that Genesis 11 is real history.

Now the whole earth had one language and one speech.

When mankind was originally made, there was only one language created. During the Tower of Babel incident, languages were confused. Presumably, people started speaking a number of completely unrelated languages. As people spread over the globe, these would develop within those languages, to give us the languages we have today.

21.1. The Rebellion

And it came to pass, as they journeyed from the east, that they found a plain in the land of Shinar, and they dwelt there. Then they said to one another, "Come, let us make bricks and bake them thoroughly." They had brick for stone, and they had asphalt for mortar. And they said, "Come, let us build ourselves a city, and a tower whose top is in the heavens; let us make a name for ourselves, lest we be scattered abroad over the face of the whole earth."

The Hebrew word referring to East is somewhat unclear. If we take the translation at face value, then the people must have migrated further East, then West again, to reach Shinar. On the other hand, the word used could be translated Eastward, which would make sense of the direction of migration. The NIV and NAS have this translation, whereas the KJV and NKJV have "from the East".

Shinar is the area between the Tigris and Euphrates rivers. It is likely that the people found this to be a very fertile area, and it perhaps reminded them of the pre-Flood Eden. Therefore, they named the rivers after two of the rivers flowing out of Eden. These present day Tigris and Euphrates are not the same as the pre-diluvian rivers of the same names. There are a number of reasons why the rivers are not the same.

- The present Tigris and Euphrates do not have a common source.
- The Flood would have destroyed all topographical features.
- The present rivers flow over sedimentary rock, laid down in the

Flood

To get a clue to what is happening in the world of Genesis 11, we need to interpret it with respect to Genesis 10. God had commanded Noah and his family to "be fruitful and multiply" (Genesis 9:7) and to fill the Earth. Now, in Genesis 11, we have the people settled in Shinar. We have already read of a great military leader, called Nimrod, who is a mighty hunter in the face of the LORD. Nimrod, we read in Genesis 10, founded the cities in the plain of Shinar. The first and most important of these was at Babylon, or Babel.

Since it is clear that Nimrod opposed the LORD, it is safe to assume that he would want to resist God's command to fill the Earth. Being a mighty military leader, we can surmise that he wanted to control the world's population himself. There are clues to this – witness his invasion of Assyria, the realm of Asshur. Add to this some information from non-Biblical accounts of Nimrod, and we can develop a picture of what must have happened.

Many legends refer to Nimrod as a tyrant, god-like ruler. His wife, according to legend, was Semiramis. Babylon appears to be the source of much of the world's paganism. People began to worship what was created rather than the creator. As an aside, after his death, Nimrod was deified by his widow. She later had an illegitimate child, Tammuz, but claimed that Tammuz was actually Nimrod re-incarnated. This legend has echoes in stories around the world, such as Horus or Krishna. Semiramis associated herself with the constellation Virgo. The constellations were probably originally a means of understanding the true gospel ("The heavens declare the glory of God" Psalm 19:1), with Virgo representing the virgin birth promised by God in Genesis 3 (the seed of the woman). Semiramis corrupted this worship, and was declared Queen of Heaven. The image of Queen of Heaven, with re-incarnated baby deity, as Madonna and Child, became common. This false worship has, unfortunately, crept into Christian churches. It would be worth reading accounts of this, and Dagon the fish-god, in Gascoigne.[1]

To return to the story of Genesis 11: Nimrod is ruling the world's first military empire from Babel. He is preventing people from scattering

---

[1] Gascoigne, M, *Forgotten History of the Western People*, Anno Mundi: 2002

across the Earth. He is pointing people away from God, and causing them to worship other gods. It is into this background that his council declare the need to build a special city, with a tower "whose top is in the heavens". It is likely that this really means a "tower to the heavens" i.e. one dedicated to the heavens, rather than one which necessarily reaches high. Such religious objects are known throughout the world, so the peoples scattered by the Babel incident must have taken with them the desire to reach the heavens by their own means, rather than a worship of God. It is possible to understand many antiquities in this light: pyramids of Egypt, Stonehenge etc. In the peoples' declaration, it is clear that they intend to resist God's command. "Let us make a name for ourselves, lest we be scattered abroad over the face of the whole earth."

21.2. The Response

But the LORD came down to see the city and the tower which the sons of men had built. And the LORD said, "Indeed the people are one and they all have one language, and this is what they begin to do; now nothing that they propose to do will be withheld from them. Come, let Us go down and there confuse their language, that they may not understand one another's speech." So the LORD scattered them abroad from there over the face of all the earth, and they ceased building the city. Therefore its name is called Babel, because there the LORD confused the language of all the earth; and from there the LORD scattered them abroad over the face of all the earth.

When the passage says "The LORD came down to see the city", this does not imply that Almighty God did not know what was going on. It is, rather, a clear indication of God's intention to do something about it. Moses received a similar response from God.

And the LORD said: "I have surely seen the oppression of My people who are in Egypt, and have heard their cry because of their taskmasters, for I know their sorrows. So I have *come down* to deliver them out of the hand of the Egyptians, and to bring them up from that land to a good and large land, to a land flowing with milk and honey, to the place of the Canaanites and the Hittites and the Amorites and the Perizzites and the Hivites and the

Jebusites."[2]

When I read about God's response to the people at Babel, I am reminded of Galatians 6:7. "Do not be deceived, God is not mocked; for whatever a man sows, that he will also reap." God's command was for mankind to fill the Earth. Mankind was attempting to resist that command. God was not to be thwarted, so He forced the people to scatter, by confusing their languages. If they had obeyed God, they would have had the whole world, but communications would have been so much easier. As it was, work on the Tower of Babel quickly came to a halt. One worker said to another, "Pass me the hammer, Jim!", but the other person heard "Accordez moi le marteau, Jacques!"[3]. It was obvious to all that they would not be able to work together.

After God confused the languages, the name Babel took on a new meaning. It is an example of onomatopoeia, a word having a meaning derived from its own sound. In English, we speak of *babblers*, a word derived from Babel.

There are some who claim that Babel means "Gate of God". This is not a problem, however, because after the Confusion of Languages, the same word-sound could mean different things in different languages.

21.3. The Genealogy of Terah

This is the genealogy of Shem: Shem was one hundred years old, and begot Arphaxad two years after the flood. After he begot Arphaxad, Shem lived five hundred years, and begot sons and daughters.

Arphaxad lived thirty–five years, and begot Salah. After he begot Salah, Arphaxad lived four hundred and three years, and begot sons and daughters.

Salah lived thirty years, and begot Eber. After he begot Eber, Salah lived

---

[2] Exodus 3:7,8 – emphasis mine

[3] Note for pedants: This was just a little joke. Obviously, French and English have both derived from the same language group, therefore would be represented by only one of the languages at Babel.

four hundred and three years, and begot sons and daughters.

Eber lived thirty–four years, and begot Peleg. After he begot Peleg, Eber lived four hundred and thirty years, and begot sons and daughters.

Peleg lived thirty years, and begot Reu. After he begot Reu, Peleg lived two hundred and nine years, and begot sons and daughters.

Reu lived thirty–two years, and begot Serug. After he begot Serug, Reu lived two hundred and seven years, and begot sons and daughters.

Serug lived thirty years, and begot Nahor. After he begot Nahor, Serug lived two hundred years, and begot sons and daughters.

Nahor lived twenty–nine years, and begot Terah. After he begot Terah, Nahor lived one hundred and nineteen years, and begot sons and daughters.

Now Terah lived seventy years, and begot Abram, Nahor, and Haran.

This is the genealogy of Terah: Terah begot Abram, Nahor, and Haran. Haran begot Lot. And Haran died before his father Terah in his native land, in Ur of the Chaldeans. Then Abram and Nahor took wives: the name of Abram's wife was Sarai, and the name of Nahor's wife, Milcah, the daughter of Haran the father of Milcah and the father of Iscah. But Sarai was barren; she had no child. And Terah took his son Abram and his grandson Lot, the son of Haran, and his daughter–in–law Sarai, his son Abram's wife, and they went out with them from Ur of the Chaldeans to go to the land of Canaan; and they came to Haran and dwelt there. So the days of Terah were two hundred and five years, and Terah died in Haran.

This genealogy appears to be of incredible importance. The structure of the genealogy is similar to that of Genesis 5. We argued that the Genesis 5 genealogy cannot contain gaps, or the meaning of the names, and the repetition of the genealogies in 1 Chronicles 1 and Luke 3 would not make sense. Because this Genesis 11 genealogy is of similar format to Genesis 5, it is reasonable to suppose that this genealogy also contains no gaps. The purpose of the genealogy appears to be to connect the events of the creation, Flood and Babel, with the known real history of Abraham. Although this work concludes with Genesis 11, this should not be used as an excuse to suppose that the first section of Genesis is of more or lesser importance than chapters 12 to 50. Indeed, it is because Genesis 12 to 50 is history, and Genesis 1 to 11 reads as the same style, that we can confidently state that Genesis 1 to 11 is also history. This does present a problem, however. Genesis 11's genealogy agrees with that of 1 Chronicles, but not with that of Luke 3. The Luke 3 account places another Cainan between Arphaxad and Salah. Sarfati explains this well:

> Note that the Greek New Testament was originally written without punctuation or spaces between words. So Luke 3:35–38 would have been originally written as below. In this manuscript, TOUKAINAN (the son of Cainan) could have been on the end of the third line:

ΤΟΥΣΑΡΟΥΧΤΟΥΡΑΓΑΥΤΟΥΦΑΛΕΓΤΟΥΕΒΕΡΤΟΥΣΑΛΑ
ΤΟΥΑΡΦΑΞΑΔΤΟΥΣΗΜΤΟΥΝΩΕΤΟΥΛΑΜΕΧ
ΤΟΥΜΑΘΟΥΣΑΛΑΤΟΥΕΝΩΧΤΟΥΙΑΡΕΔΤΟΥΜΑΛΕΛΕΗΛ*ΤΟΥΚΑΙΝΑΙ*
ΤΟΥΕΝΩΣΤΟΥΣΗΘΤΟΥΑΔΑΜΤΟΥΘΕΟΥ

> But suppose an early copyist of Luke's gospel was copying the first line, but his eyes glanced at the end of the third line at TOUKAINAN. Then he would have written it on the first line as well:

ΤΟΥΣΑΡΟΥΧΤΟΥΡΑΓΑΥΤΟΥΦΑΛΕΓΤΟΥΕΒΕΡΤΟΥΣΑΛΑ*ΤΟΥΚΑΙΝΑ*
ΤΟΥΑΡΦΑΞΑΔΤΟΥΣΗΜΤΟΥΝΩΕΤΟΥΛΑΜΕΧ
ΤΟΥΜΑΘΟΥΣΑΛΑΤΟΥΕΝΩΧΤΟΥΙΑΡΕΔΤΟΥΜΑΛΕΛΕΗΛ*ΤΟΥΚΑΙΝΑ*
ΤΟΥΕΝΩΣΤΟΥΣΗΘΤΟΥΑΔΑΜΤΟΥΘΕΟΥ

> In English, keeping the same line formatting, and with italics indicating words added by the translators which were understood in the Greek, so the passage makes sense in English:

> *The son of Serug, the son of Reu, the son of Peleg, the son of Eber, the son of Shelah, the son of Cainan, the son of Arphaxad, the son of Shem, the son of Noah, the son of Lamech, the son of Methuselah, the son of Enoch, the*

son of Jared, the son of Mahalalel, the son of Cainan, the son of Enosh, the son of Seth, the son of Adam, the son of God.[4]

With this convincing explanation accepted, we now have a timescale for the patriarch's after the Flood, to compare with that of before the Flood.

	Birth (after Flood)	Age of father	Age at death	Death (a Flood)
Noah	-600		950	
Shem	-98		600	
Arphaxad	2	100	438	
Salah	37	35	433	
Eber	67	30	464	
Peleg	101	34	239	
Reu	131	30	239	
Serug	163	32	230	
Nahor	193	30	148	
Terah	222	29	205	
Abram	292	70	175	

From this timescale, it can be seen that Shem outlived Abraham. It can also be seen that the ages at death is declining. Clearly, the post-diluvian world allows more genetic mutations to form, thus reducing the lifespan.

---

[4] Sarfati, J. *Cainan: How do you explain the difference between Luke 3:36 and Genesis 11:12?*, http://www.answersingenesis.org/docs/3748.asp

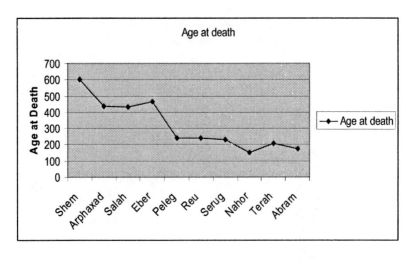

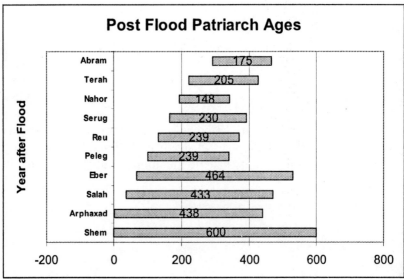

The older patriarchs must have been well known to the ancients. Indeed, some non-Biblical accounts have it that the mysterious Melchizedek, or Genesis 14, is actually Shem.[5]

---

[5] Morris, H., *The Genesis Record*, Evangelical Press: 1976, p320

The importance of these genealogies of Shem and Terah is that they connect the events of the early history of the world with the events, or which we are more familiar. The genealogies are historical records, and should be taken as such. It is these records that help to verify the hermeneutical status of all that has gone before. The early chapters of Genesis are not poetry, nor are they mythology. They are genuine history, and deserve to be taught as such.

Appendix: The Gospel According to Saint Moses

I have taken very seriously the issue of Creation Evangelism. My own contribution to the effort is a short booklet, entitled "The Gospel According to Saint Moses", which I have printed and given out at my talks on creationism. The text of this booklet is included here, as an appendix.

■■

Moses was a saint, according to the Bible's definition of sainthood.

> By faith Moses, when he became of age, refused to be called the son of Pharaoh's daughter, choosing rather to suffer affliction with the people of God than to enjoy the passing pleasures of sin, esteeming the reproach of Christ greater riches than the treasures in Egypt; for he looked to the reward. (Hebrews 11:24-26)

Hebrews shows that Moses had a living faith in the Christ who was to come. Like the other Old Testament saints mentioned in Hebrews 11, he was saved as we are, by faith in the Saviour Messiah. The only difference is that Moses was saved before Jesus had actually walked this earth.

Moses did meet Jesus, however.

> Now after six days Jesus took Peter, James, and John his brother, led them up on a high mountain by themselves; and He was transfigured before them. His face shone like the sun, and His clothes became as white as the light. And behold, Moses and Elijah appeared to them, talking with Him. (Matthew 17:1-3)

The ordinariness, with which Matthew discusses the supernatural is an element missing from today's gospel. As I write this article, churches where I live, in Wales, are preparing to celebrate the centenary of the 1904 revival. The wonder of the 1904 revival to me is that revival hasn't happened since. When the revivalists were seeking a move of the Holy Spirit, they knew such a power of God either from their own lifetimes, or from the lifetimes of their parents. For the preceding two hundred years or so, there had been many times locally or nationally that the people of Wales had experienced such a move of the Holy Spirit. It is said that on one occasion, the revivalist Evan Roberts stood in the pulpit for an hour in silence, but men and women still cried out to be saved. Why do we not see such things today? It is because society has changed, and with it, the effectiveness of the gospel.

I am not asking for the gospel to be changed for today's society. Perish the thought. But in days past, certain elements of the gospel could be assumed, which today need to be explicitly stated. Evan Roberts could stand in silence, because he knew the people were ready for repentance. They knew what repentance was. They knew they were sinners, because they knew what the Bible said about sin. And they knew the way of salvation was through Jesus Christ – they just hadn't trodden that road yet for themselves. In 1904 thousands of Welsh people gave their hearts to the Saviour that they already knew about in their minds. The head knowledge was not enough to save them, but it was enough to provide the map for the road ahead.

Today's society does not have that road map. Ordinary people today do not know the Bible. Indeed, many, if not most, ordinary Christians do not know the Bible well.

That is why today we need the Gospel according to Saint Moses, and that is what this article attempts to tell you. The Gospel according to Saint Moses hits society at the point where society believes it has undermined the Bible. Society ignores the Bible, because it believes it has been superseded. Christians have conceded the truth of portions of the Bible, thus undermining the foundations of the Gospel. The Gospel according to Saint Moses seeks to restore that foundation. It is not a new Gospel. It is not a different Gospel. Indeed, it is the oldest possible account of the Gospel, rooted as it is in the first few chapters of the first book that Moses wrote – the book of Genesis. In presenting the Gospel in this way, I am not attempting to verify the account of creation scientifically – though I have done so elsewhere, and am happy to do so on other occasions. Rather I take the assumption of the truth of Genesis and build a self-consistent account of the Gospel. If you don't accept the truth of Genesis, you can at least acknowledge the internal consistency of the argument, and then look further at why an increasing number of Bible scholars take the book of Genesis to be literal, historical fact.

God made the world for people

A key phrase appears over and over again during the six days of creation. Here it is in Gen 1:4 "And God saw the light, that *it was good*". What was so good about the light? Here it is again in verse 12 – "And God saw that it was good".

To understand what was so good about these acts of creation, we need to look at how God felt when creation was complete.

Partway through Day 6, He again observes: "And God made the beast of the earth according to its kind, cattle according to its kind, and everything that creeps on the earth according to its kind. And God saw that it was good." But at the end of the same day, we read: "Then God saw everything that He had made, and indeed it was very good." What was formerly just good has now become *very good*. The difference is that now God has made people. His creation is complete because He has made man in His own image. Creation was good before, because God was preparing the world for mankind. Now that He has made mankind, He describes the world as very good. This shows us that the whole purpose of creation was for us – God made the world and the universe for us to inhabit and to enjoy a relationship with Him. He made it so that mankind could commune with Him, walking together in the Garden, in the "cool of the day".

God made man and woman

There is a significant difference between the way Adam was made and the way Eve was made. Adam was directly created by God, from the dust of the earth. Eve was made out of Adam. This means that Adam originally contained all Eve's genetic material.

There are those who believe that God created by evolution. Adam and Eve, if they existed, were the first evolved hominids. But if this were so, then Jesus could not be a representative Saviour for women, and we need to have a female Messiah. However, the first Adam was our representative in the Garden. He was also Eve's representative. In 1 Timothy 2:14, we read: "And Adam was not deceived, but the woman being deceived, fell into transgression." Eve was deceived by the serpent, and she sinned. Her sin was hers, and hers alone. But Adam took the fruit and ate, even though he was not deceived. In other words, he knew what he was doing. He sinned as our representative, so his sin was not just his own, but imputed to the whole human race.

Just as sin came into the world through one man, so the destruction of sin and death comes from one man – Jesus Christ. The Apostle Paul argues this point very clearly in Romans 5 and 1 Corinthians 15.

Sin came by yielding to temptation

Notice the way that the serpent, who is Satan, deceived Eve.

He started by planting doubt in Eve's mind. "Did God really say...?" If we doubt what God has said in His word, then we have no basis for our faith. That is why it is so important to believe what God says in the Bible.

Notice next that Eve misquotes God. "You shall not eat it, nor shall you touch it, lest you die." God did not tell Adam and Eve not to touch the fruit. Adding to God's word is serious. There are church groups today who have added to God's word, the Bible. Just as it is serious to disbelieve the Bible, it is dangerous to add to it. Eve's additions were probably in error. She simply hadn't listened carefully enough to what God said. We need to know God's word. In Psalm 119:11, we read: "Your word I have hidden in my heart, that I might not sin against You!" A good knowledge of the Bible is very helpful. There was a time when most Christians could recite words of scripture. Not today. People do not learn verses of scripture. This is a shame, because of the tremendous help there is to be found in knowing the word.

Next notice that Satan directly contradicts God:- "You will not surely die". Once we have opened our minds to the possibility of doubt, and have insufficient knowledge of God's word, or added to it, then we find it possible to directly oppose God.

Through this sad catalogue of events, Eve sinned, followed by Adam, who sinned with his eyes open, so to speak.

Sin separates us from God

Immediately, Adam and Eve were separated from God. As God walked in the Garden in the cool of the day, Adam and Eve hid.

Today, we do not have full fellowship with God, because we are guilty of sin. This guilt makes us uncomfortable even in the presence of a godly man or woman, who themselves are sinners. But in the presence of God, we cannot stand

We try to cover our own guilt

Adam and eve did this by sowing fig leaves together. These garments, they hoped, would cover their nakedness.

We also try to justify ourselves before God. "I've tried to live a good life, I've done the best I can, I've worked hard for church." God sees through these things, and we stand before Him naked and ashamed.

God covered Adam and Eve's guilt differently. He gave them garments of skin. (Gen 3:21). Yet, before that point, no animals had ever died. God deliberately killed animals to make more suitable clothes to cover Adam and Eve's nakedness. The book of Hebrews reminds us "And according to the law almost all things are purified with blood, and without shedding of blood there is no remission. (Hebrews 9:22). When the sacrificial system was instituted, Moses sprinkled the people with the blood of the sacrifices, declaring "This is the blood of the covenant..." In the same way, Jesus described His blood as the "Blood of the New Covenant". Jesus's perfect sacrifice was once for all. Adam and Eve did not know about this yet, but still God had to shed blood to cover their nakedness.

Our own efforts at religion do not cover our nakedness. Only the sacrifice of Jesus can do this completely for us.

God promised Jesus

As God cursed the serpent, so He promised "I will put enmity between you and the woman, And between your seed and her Seed; He shall bruise your head, And you shall bruise His heel." The Seed of the Woman was to save us – by crushing the serpents head, even though the serpent would bruise his heel. The sufferings of Jesus were great. We don't need a film to tell us that. But Satan was not to have the victory, because he would only bruise Jesus's heel. Jesus is the promised Seed of the Woman. How can we be sure? It is because only men have seed. Children are described in the Bible as the seed of the father. In Genesis 21:13, God says to Abraham "Yet I will also make a nation of the son of the bondwoman, because he is your seed." So God was promising one day that there would be a Seed of the Woman – that is as clear a prediction of the Virgin Birth as we need. One day, says God, there will be a descendent of Adam and Eve, who does not have an earthly father, but who does have an earthly mother. Only Jesus fits that description.

Conclusion

From the first three chapters of Genesis, we learn:

1. God made the world
2. God made the world for people
3. God made the world so that we could inhabit it, work it and have communion with Him
4. Communion with God was broken by sin
5. Sin can often come about if we disbelieve God, doubt His word or misquote Him.
6. We are all sinners, because we are all of Adam's race.

7. We cannot undo our own sins. We cannot get ourselves right with God.
8. God Himself has found a way for us to have restored fellowship with Him. It is by the shedding of blood.
9. It is by the shedding of the perfect blood of Jesus Christ, the Lamb of God, that we can be perfectly saved.

Genesis shows us why God made the world, how God made the world and who He made it for. It shows us that we are designed to have fellowship with Him. It also shows that we do not have that fellowship. We can, however, have fellowship again with God, by coming to faith in Jesus Christ.

He was in the world, and the world was made through Him, and the world did not know Him. He came to His own, and His own did not receive Him. But as many as received Him, to them He gave the right to become children of God, to those who believe in His name: who were born, not of blood, nor of the will of the flesh, nor of the will of man, but of God. (John 1:10-13)

If you haven't yet become a Christian, by faith in Jesus Christ, I urge you to do so. Maybe you need to pray with someone. Find a good local church that believes the Bible – unfortunately not all churches believe the Bible to be completely true.

A prayer

*Lord God, thank You for making me. Thank you for making me and wanting fellowship with me. I'm sorry for all my sins, remembering some of them at this moment. I want to turn away from them, and have fellowship with You. Thank you for sending Your precious Son, Jesus, to die as a punishment for **my** sins. I receive Him now and turn to You, Lord God, in repentance and faith. Amen.*

Bibliography

author	title	publisher	year
Batten, D. and Sarfati, J.	*How did fish and plants survive the Genesis Flood?*	http://www.answersingenesis .org/docs/444.asp	
Berndt, Chard	*The Pre-Fall Mortality of Aquatic Autotrophs and Other Designated Nephesh kinds,*	*CRSQ* Vol 40 No 2 pp85-89 September 2003	
Cooper, W	*After the Flood*	New Wine Press	1995
Cousteau, J	*The Ocean World of Jacques Cousteau - Oasis In Space*	Angus & Robertson	
D.R. Humphreys	*Starlight and Time, Solving the Puzzle of Distant Starlight in a Young Universe*	Master Books	1994
Day One Magazine			
Fields, W.W.	*Unformed and Unfilled, A Critique of the Gap Theory*	Burgener Enterprises	1976
Frair, W	*Baraminology— Classification of Created Organisms*	*CRSQ Vol 37 No 2 pp82-91* September 2000	
Garner, P.	*The Age of the Earth: Geology and the Deluge*	http://www.amen.org.uk/ch/s cience/flodpg/flodpg3.htm 2000	
Gascoigne, M	*Forgotten History of the Western People*	Anno Mundi	2002
Ham, K., Sarfati, J.,	*The Answers Book*	Master Books	2000

Bibliography

author	title	publisher	year
Wieland, C.			
Ham, Ken	*One Blood: The Biblical Answer to Racism*	Master Books	
Hawking, S.W.,	*A Brief History of Time*	Transworld	1988
Lewis, C.S.	*Miracles*	Collins	1947
López, R.E		TJ 12(3) 1998: 347-357	
McIntosh, A.	*A. Genesis for today*	DayOne	1997
McIntosh, A., Taylor, S., Edmondson, T.	*McIntosh, Taylor and Edmondson reply to Flood Models*	TJ 14(3) 2000:80–82	
Morris, H.M.	*The Genesis Record*	Baker Book House	1976
Morris, H.M.	*The Revelation Record*	Tyndale	1983
Morris, H.M.	*The Bible Has the Answer*	Master Books	1987
Morris, J.D.	*The Young Earth*	Master Books	1998
Poole, M.	*Commentary of the Bible*		
Robinson, S.J.	*Interpreting the Fossil Record*	http://www.noahsarkzoofarm.co.uk/research/interpretations.shtml 2004	
Sarfati, J		TJ 17(3) 2003: 14ff	
Sarfati, J.	*reply to letter Cainan: How do you explain the difference between Luke 3:36 and Genesis 11:12?*	http://www.answersingenesis.org/docs/3748.asp	

Just Six Days

author	title	publisher	year
Schaeffer, F.A.	*How Should We Then Live? The Rise and Decline of Western Thought and Culture,*	Crossway	1976
Setterfield, B. and Norman, T.,	*The Atomic Constants, Light and Time*	http://www.setterfield.org/report/report.html 1987	
Taylor, C.V.	*Did the Mountains Really Rise According to Psalm 104:8?*	TJ 12 (3) 1998: 312-313	
Tipler, F.J.	*The Physics of Immortality*	Macmillan	1994
Whitcomb, J.C. and Morris, H.M.	*The Genesis Flood*	Baker Book House	1961
Woodmorappe, J.	*Noah's Ark: A Feasibility Study*	ICR	1996

Printed in the United Kingdom
by Lightning Source UK Ltd.
102951UKS00001B/25-96